A Real Estate Mogul's Blueprint for Success

By Jerry L. Wallace

CAREER PRESS The Career Press, Inc.
Franklin Lakes, NJ

DEALMAKER
EDITED BY DIANNA WALSH
TYPESET BY MICHAEL FITZGIBBON
Cover design by Rob Johnson/Johnson Design
Printed in the U.S.A. by Book-mart Press

To order this title, please call toll-free 1-800-CAREER-1 (NJ and Canada: 201-848-0310) to order using VISA or MasterCard, or for further information on books from Career Press.

CAREER
PRESS

The Career Press, Inc., 3 Tice Road, PO Box 687,
Franklin Lakes, NJ 07417
www.careerpress.com

Library of Congress Cataloging-in-Publication Data

Wallace, Jerry L., 1940-
    Dealmaker : a real estate mogul's blueprint for success / by Jerry L. Wallace
        p. cm.
    Includes bibliographical references and index.
    ISBN-13: 978-1-56414-949-7
    ISBN-10: 1-56414-949-8
        1. Businesspeople—United States—Biography. 2. Real estate developers—United States—Biography. 3. Real estate development—United States. 4. Success in business—United States. I. Title. II. Title: Deal maker. III. Title: Real estate mogul's blueprint for success.

HC102.5.W348W35 2007
333.33092—dc22

                                                2007016598

Dedication

I dedicate this book to Antone "Larry" Hutter, my mentor and beloved friend. Thank you, Larry.

To my wife, Josette, who has endured my long hours and many days of work. I love you.

And to Rodney Bell, for his insistence that I tell my story, so others may learn.

Contents

IV: Tools for Success

Foreword

During an interview, Larry King asked Bill Gates to what did he attribute his enormous success. He replied, "Larry, I was in the right place at the right time. And luck has a lot to do with that." He went on to state that what he meant by luck is that he was in the right place at the right time, and he was lucky to have the vision to see it and the resolve to take "massive and immediate action."

This exchange brought to my mind very provocative thoughts. I wondered about all the many other people who Gates said were also in that "right place at that right time" and either didn't see or didn't act on the very same opportunity that ultimately created the wealthiest man in the world. How profound, I thought. I wrestled with this very unique concept of luck as redefined by Bill Gates. Could his enormous wealth really be due to the fact that he had vision and resolve? I knew a lot of people with vision and resolve. Could it just as likely have been any of them standing in his shoes? Perhaps a close friend? Someone in my family? Could even *I* have done it? Could I have used my vision and resolve to become the wealthiest man in the world? Now that question brought me back to reality quickly. That answer was simple: No.

Actually, I think the answer was, "No, not a chance." You see, in his inspiring oratory Bill Gates left out a little fundamental requisite to his luck: his knowledge! He was right about being in the right place at the right time, but what I suspect mostly attracted such luck was the fact that he went to Harvard (prelaw), owned QDOS, wrote programs, and had direct access to IBM's president and Apple's highest corporate offices. In other words, he had acquired some very uncommon knowledge and access, which allowed him to see and act massively on that incredible opportunity. That made more sense.

That is what this book is designed to do. It provides the exceptional individual with enough uncommon knowledge to recognize incredible opportunities when they present themselves. The information provided can guide you into reaching even your most ambitious goals. You will learn how to conceptualize, propose, and deliver the win-win deal. If you follow the author's instructions, this book will become your introduction to an uncommon access.

Before you begin, let's get back to Mr. Gates. When he mentions to Larry King that what sets him apart is his "luck," he admits that there were a lot of people at the same place he was and that a lot of people had the same vision. The big difference was, Mr. Gates had vision and saw the potential that was there.

I would dare to say that others see it now! I would be so bold to state that Mr. Gates is no longer even close to being alone in his expertise; in fact, his once visionary knowledge is no longer that uncommon in his field. There are others. I strongly submit to you that he is not without peers.

Yet he still remains without equals! Why is he still the richest man in the world?

Why isn't the brilliant computer geek that lives across the street now the richest person in the world? What's Bill Gates got that all of us don't?

Well, let's see. For starters, he has more than 1,000 licenses, patents, and copyright protections. It's legally defined as "intellectual property." In other words, by law the systems, the operations, and the protocols are his trade secrets and he doesn't have to share them with you. And any replication without express written permission, which you'll never get, will get you some serious federal visitors.

Bill Gates is not alone. No competitive corporation ever wants to reveal the real secrets of its trade! Until now.

The secrets and systems written in this book are the same ones that made Jerry Wallace successful. He has held nothing back. There are no links to our Website for the real information. The instructions that he has given are the same ones that he has taught and continues to teach to his agents and staff. He has laid out for you in a step-by-step system what you can do to become successful beyond your wildest dreams and enjoy real wealth that lasts a lifetime. He includes his own personal insights on deal making; he includes copies of the exact forms, contracts, and proposals that he uses routinely.

Yes, the systems are his; they are proven and can make you as wealthy as the author.

They are yours to learn and to share with others to enjoy many of the successes that he has enjoyed.

I know the author. I have watched his public and private holdings increase phenomenally in less than five years. From skillful win-win deal making, his holdings have blossomed into an ever-expanding conglomerate with end-value projects estimated to be in the billions. Jerry Wallace has been labeled the consummate dealmaker. He has set every major record in the area of preconstruction condominium sales. He is the architect of the industry, its trendsetter, and its pioneer. His knowledge of skillful deal making is second to none, and he is one of the most publicized single developers in the country. His projects range from the incredible 765-unit luxury Laketown Wharf condominiums, in which he received one of the largest loans ever granted to a private developer, to his various namesake WallaceTown themed resorts. In 2004, his agreement to purchase the town of Cornudas, Texas, granted him the singular distinction of being the only individual in the United States to privately own an entire town. I think that one was just for bragging rights.

What he doesn't brag about is this: Never one to follow, just days after Katrina struck, Jerry led a coalition of developers into the hurricane-ravaged communities with promises to rebuild the Gulf Coast bigger and better. His staff personally delivered immediate supplies and donations to the victims. He followed up this with a personal tour of the area with Miss America 2005, to aid in fundraising, raise awareness, and show support for the relentless rescue workers. Summarizing his approach to conducting business, Jerry would say, "All you have to do is step up to the plate."

Rodney Bell
President, Jerry Wallace Developments, LLC

Preface

Confidence, determination, and reputation are the keys to success in anything that you do. The first big project that I completed was enormous: a $250 million Gulf-front condominium project called Majestic Beach Towers I & II, containing 565 individual units with some commercial.

Even though I had not yet acquired even the first parcel of land, I told my new associate, Rodney Bell, who has since been an amazing colleague and friend, exactly what I was going to build and when it would be completed. It was then that I laid out for him my entire plan and the enormity of the Majestic project. As I meticulously showed him the project's boundaries, he tells others how amazed he was that this project covered up many properties and businesses, and how he was surprised that so many long time entrenched property owners *had* agreed to sell me their land.

Today, as the president of my development company, he often recounts that first meeting. Everyone thinks he is exaggerating because, very shortly after my statements, we agreed to work together. His first responsibility: to go along with me as I *introduced* myself to the *then* owners.

And he witnessed as all that I predicted with confidence about the Majestic Beach project came to pass

This was the very first project in which I had all the control and financial responsibility as a developer. After assembling several contiguous parcels of Gulf-front and non-Gulf-front properties and convincing an architect to do the preliminary building layout and floor plans for no up-front money, I began putting together a preliminary pro forma to determine how much money I needed and when. Now that I had the property optioned and the drawings started, there was no turning back on this project that everyone said was impossible for me to do. In fact, most developers of many years in the business would consider this a project of a lifetime. My next project was Shores of Panama at $300 million, followed by Laketown Wharf at $350 million.

Even before I had the first parcel under option, I told my new associate, Rodney Bell, who has since been an amazing colleague and friend, exactly what was going to be built and when it would be completed. All that I told him has now come to pass.

Amazingly, the project went extremely well for being my first. I sold out of property prior to beginning the construction. This came as a result of the confidence and conviction you must have to do what I do.

This book was written with the intention of instilling confidence in you and to teach you to obtain a sustained drive to succeed in what you have set as your goal. A person is only limited by what they believe they can't do, however, there is always a way and all you have to do is "step up to the plate!"

I

THE SECRET OF MY SUCCESS

CHAPTER 1

ACQUIRING KNOWLEDGE

Whatever you truly believe you are—you are.

An old maxim says, "Never stop learning." Consider Theodore Roosevelt, who died with a book under his pillow, consuming the ideas of others until the very last.

The thirst for knowledge is especially important in the field of real estate, the theme of the book you're now holding in your hands. But real estate, and we'll be getting to that topic in a moment, hardly has a monopoly on the acquisition of knowledge.

Let me explain. Knowledge, whether inherent or acquired, is equal to power in any business. It's the surest way to gain the respect and attention of your audience, no matter who they are. Being educated about your product allows you, the entrepreneur, to overcome all kinds of obstacles on the road to success. When you're "in the know," you have anticipated the hurdles, questions, and/or concerns that affect you and your clients, which transforms them from roadblocks to merely other steps in your plan.

Being thoroughly educated about the project you are marketing will help to establish a philosophy for the overall way you do business. Out of this is born integrity, which means remaining true to yourself and to your employees and customers.

> **Knowledge + hard work + integrity = success.**

What does this all have to do with real estate? It's fairly simple, really. Horatio Alger, when he discovered gold in California, proclaimed, "Go West!" Today I believe there's a similar fortune to be made in real estate, so it's important to be educated about the real estate business and your own projects!

What do I want you to take away from this book? Ideally, you'll put it down and go out into the world and become a millionaire through investing in real estate. Furthermore, you'll know how you can grow and secure your investments to become permanently wealthy from real estate, as I have done. I've spent the past four years creating a nine-figure net worth by applying the techniques from all my years as a real estate investor, the "blueprint" that I will lay out in this book.

Above all else, the book is intended to show an average person how he or she can use a real estate license to acquire great wealth in a short span of time. By following my simple plan, with hard work, acquired knowledge, and my proven sales techniques, anyone can become wealthy, possibly even become a power broker.

During the years, I've watched people come and go in this business. The people who left the business were those who failed to plan or failed to work. In real estate, you must both know your objective and put in the time to see it through.

Why Real Estate?

Well, why not? It's the best way to get rich that I've ever found. And believe me, yours truly has been around. I've been an aluminum siding salesman, cost estimator, builder, investment banker, stockbroker, oil man, real estate salesman, and real estate developer. So why, after years of experience in a wide range of industries, did I choose real estate as my profession? In all my travels, I have found that real estate—preconstruction condominium sales specifically— is the most rewarding, most secure, and most prolific investment in the United States today, and I believe it will be for sometime to come.

The reasons are simple:

- America's wealth is and always has been secured by real estate.

- Most fortunes in America have been amassed through real estate investment.

- Owning real estate offers tremendous tax advantages.

- Real estate values rarely experience dramatic negative swings.

- Real estate is a commodity that rarely drops to zero in value, and one of the very few commodities you can actually purchase and begin with equity, especially if you have a real estate license.

What other commodities can boast these characteristics?

The most common question I encounter from potential customers or investors in my projects is "When will prices stop going up?" Condominium prices have been rising steadily for the last decade at least, and investors want to know where the ceiling in this market is.

I focus a great deal of my time on the Florida real estate market. In my opinion, peak prices for condos in Florida won't be reached until we catch up with the rest of the world. In other words, if you go to the Cayman Islands, Hilton Head Island, Vail, and so on, and check the prices per square foot in those and similar resorts, you'll find that the Gulf Coast and other areas in Florida are only at one-third to one-half of their prices. With beaches that rival any others in North America, I see no reason for prices in Florida to stop rising.

I don't think the upward climb will stop until underpriced areas reach a competitive price level, and even then I expect it all to continue to rise together. So we may never reach that peak. Think about it for a moment: There is a finite amount of real estate on the Gulf shores. There are 76 million Baby Boomers in this country. One is turning 55 every seven seconds for the next 10 years, many of whom have saved up all their lives with the dream of buying a waterfront property where they can retire. If 25 percent of them buy resort property, that represents a demand for 19 million units.

Simply put, I can think of no logical reason for the value of these properties to go down.

Busting Myths: The Structure of the Deal

You've often heard that the three keys to success in real estate are *location, location, location*!

A nice little mantra, but not necessarily accurate. In my book, you're far better off to ignore this until you've analyzed *the deal, the deal, the deal*! As a visionary who dreams up real estate projects and a go-between working with both investors and developers, I have learned that my "product" is ultimately not the property itself; it's the deal and your vision that make it all possible and successful.

That's why, when I advise you to get educated about your product, I'm talking about the deal.

I consider myself a Realtor first and a developer second. Now don't get me wrong. I'm not saying that you have to become a developer to be what the business media likes to call a *power broker*. But in order to become a power broker, you need to study and understand what a developer does and how he does it. Having an extensive amount of experience and knowledge in this industry, I've cracked the code, so to speak, and I am now in a position to share all this knowledge with real estate enthusiasts who have the same passion I do. That's exactly what I intend to do in this book.

First, Make a Plan

An old saying goes: "Yard by yard, life is hard. But inch by inch, it's a cinch." It may sound hokey, but it's good advice to beginning real estate investors. The key to success in the real estate market is not just having the institutional knowledge that I discussed in the beginning of this book, but also having the patience and ability to lay out a step-by-step plan, one you can follow and use time and again on the road to real estate success.

Try starting out with a simple task: Craft a plan and write it down. Think through all the stages of your real estate investing strategy and try to identify the people, places, and things you'll need to carry it out to the end (for example, contractors, developers, bankers, customers, mentors, capital, and so on).

Then, show your plan to someone trustworthy who has been successful in another field for his or her review. The field itself doesn't matter, because you'll find that success is success and tends to reflect the same qualities regardless of someone's area or specific expertise. Success happens to people who are prepared for it, those who know how to identify the right steps, questions, and potential obstacles along their path, and who possess the confidence to forge ahead and overcome them.

Therefore, a successful person, even from a completely different career field, can be extremely helpful in asking questions that target the logic of your proposal, regardless of whether he or she agrees with the specific concept or procedures involved.

When sharing your goals, choose someone who is an optimist. In the real estate investing world there is simply no room for negative thinking. You should be careful to avoid negative friends or family who, for instance, advise you to shy away from risks. There's an old saying that a turtle only makes progress when he sticks his neck out. Sure, the lights ahead of you are rarely all green, but in order to be successful, you have to take some risks. A good advisor or mentor will help you identify an appropriate level of risk and limit your amount of exposure. Much of this risk exposure can be eliminated with the right structure of the deal, which we will cover later in this book.

Whatever the specifics of your particular real estate strategy, your goal is to make a plan and stick to it. It helps to take things in stages: begin each business day early with a specific agenda, and write it down!

Know Your Product

Over my years in business, I've observed that some people are natural salespeople while others couldn't sell a cheeseburger to a starving man. That's okay. We each have our own talents. But some people could easily learn the art of sales by following the example of others with a proven success record. Even those born with the natural ability to sell must build a substantial foundation of knowledge about each product they wish to sell. In order to build that base of knowledge, you need to study your project, and then apply your knowledge just as you would the steps of a recipe. All the ingredients must be in place.

For example, when I first decided to study the Florida condominium market I set out to tour each and every condominium complex in the region. I traveled from the west end of the local beach region, called Okaloosa Island, Florida, to the far eastern outskirts of the area in Sea Grove Beach.

I made appointments and personally visited each and every condominium complex in the area.

I:

- Previewed the units that were being offered for sale or rent.

- Took careful notes on each complex and learned of all the amenities each had to offer.

- Learned about the short falls of the various locations.

- Made a point of talking to the individual rental managers and real estate agents representing each property.

I also took note of important statistics, such as how many units were owner-occupied. How many were on the rental program? What were the daily, weekly, monthly, and annual leasing rates for each unit in the condominium complex? How many of the rentals were vacant? What was the average selling price for each comparable unit? This is a small sample of the information I needed to gather to prepare plans for my own project and give it the best chance for success.

Using all the information I had gathered at the various complexes, I compiled lists (that's the "writing things down" part I mentioned earlier) and made comparisons among the different developments. I kept detailed notes on the square footage of units, size of unit balconies, and the overall amenities of each project.

Armed with all this information, I felt well prepared to answer the questions most likely to arise from my own potential customers. The best way to overcome objections from a new customer is to anticipate probable questions and prepare your answers in advance. You can formulate these answers by practicing with your business colleagues and friends.

In the real estate market, your number one priority when meeting potential customers is to impress them with your product knowledge without offending them by acting like a know-it-all. A great first impression is vital to the initial sale and helps to maintain a continued relationship. And as anyone will tell you, you only have one chance to make that first impression. The first 60 seconds in meeting someone is the impression you'll leave for the long haul.

Making that impression count is all about having confidence. Preparation is the key to confidence. If you walk into a meeting feeling prepared, you will radiate confidence, and that will show through to your clients. Candidness counts, too. If a client ever asks a question for which you honestly don't have the answer, you should say so immediately, but assure them you'll find the answer, and be sure to follow up when you find that answer. People don't expect you to know everything on your own, but they do expect and appreciate honesty.

If you don't demonstrate confidence in your ability, then naturally, neither will your potential clients. And if they don't feel confident in you, your chance of a sale is extremely slim.

Gaining "Foundational" Knowledge

Now that I've advised you to go out and gain knowledge, you're probably wondering what specific knowledge? I'll go into more detail later in the book, but first and foremost you will need to acquire what is referred to as "foundational" knowledge. This basically means you'll learn about the business of real estate.

The plan I will lay out is aimed at newcomers to real estate, those looking to get started in an industry that can seem almost overwhelmingly broad in scale.

As your experience and interests develop, you can learn and apply much more to your own career. I would advise anyone serious about real estate to view it as a lifelong educational process.

In this book, I'll try to give you what you need to get started. Even still, taking some additional, basic courses can save you much time and effort in your working day. Among the most helpful skills for you to have are:

- Typing.

- Speed reading.

- Shorthand.

- Computer basics.

- Accounting skills.

All of these skills are probably offered in your area in the form of coursework and online training sessions, and they don't require any advanced education. Not only does this kind of knowledge, skill, and expertise save you time, it saves you money and aggravation, and it will increase your efficiency in responding immediately to everyday business demands.

On a personal note: Although I work with others, I have aimed to be completely self-sufficient in every aspect of my business, so I don't have to depend on any other person to get things done. In my experience, I've found that dependency almost always causes delays and/or miscalculations in your everyday business.

Granted, this doesn't mean you have to go it alone. There's a difference between dependency and delegation, which is allowing qualified and trusted associates to help you achieve your goals. Dependency, in my interpretation, means you're relying on someone else for the core knowledge or physical abilities to complete a task you cannot adequately perform yourself.

But dependency can go too far. You never want to put yourself in a position where other people can essentially hold you hostage by knowing more about managing your own business than you do. What would happen if a key member of your staff asks for a raise or simply leaves? If you don't thoroughly understand what that person does, his or her absence could bring your business to a grinding halt for days or possibly weeks.

Your goal should be to know how to manage every aspect of your business. You should always be prepared for the loss of anyone on your team. You don't have to be an expert, but by learning the logic and the basic skills required to perform your own accounting, run computer programs, and so on, you'll have the knowledge you need to thrive on your own, if you need to.

CHAPTER 2

THE SECRET OF MY SUCCESS

Let's talk a bit about time management. As business guru Peter Drucker says, "Time is the scarcest resource, and unless it is managed nothing else can be managed."

Consequently, time management is essential in any successful business. You've heard the adage that you get out of work what you put into it. The best way to get the most of your workday is to spend it as efficiently as possible.

Because everybody has different work styles, schedules, and strengths, it's worth asking yourself, "When do I perform at my best?" Are you an early morning person or do you prefer to burn the midnight oil? Consider your own personality. What kind of work setting or schedule best motivates you and helps you to succeed? Naturally, you'll want to focus the better part of your energy during that time.

Personally, I have determined that my most productive hours are from 5 o'clock in the morning until 3 o'clock in the afternoon. That's when I choose to do most of my work, when I know that my mind will be fresh, clear, and functioning at 100 percent.

You need to determine when your mind and body are functioning at their peak so you can use that time to the best advantage. Even if they're not typical hours, you can always catch up on rest during your low-performance periods. As a real estate entrepreneur, you can afford to be flexible with your time, which doesn't mean slacking, just organizing your schedule according to your own body clock. Take advantage of this freedom to help you work at your best.

Time and Motion Study

I once took a study course called "Time and Motion Study," which I thought rather boring at the time. Little did I know that this course would play a big part in the successes I would have later in life. It was then that I learned all about *therbligs*, which the dictionary defines as "any of the basic elements involved in completing a given manual operation or task that can be subjected to analysis." In simple terms, a "therblig" is any of the individual, measurable movements made while you are performing a physical task.

By studying some of the routine tasks you perform and breaking them down into therbligs, you can identify better and faster ways of physically performing a job. This will allow you to get many more things accomplished in the same amount of time.

For example, you might be in the habit of tapping your pencil for a period before you begin to write, answer the phone, and so on. Each tap of your pencil represents two therbligs—one movement up and one down. Eliminating those movements saves you just a little bit of time in your day.

That's a very small example, but on a larger scale, thinking in terms of therbligs helps you become aware of other time-wasting activities or inefficiencies throughout your day. Right now, they're most likely unconscious. Once you become more aware of your daily habits, you can seek to eliminate any that don't contribute to your productivity or reorganize them as it makes sense. When are you most likely to be interrupted in the course of your day? When are customers more likely to respond to your messages? Can you consolidate your phone calls, faxes, appointments, and so on, into one productive period and save yourself valuable time?

This is the same principle Henry Ford applied when introducing the assembly line to the automobile industry; a revolution that made the assembly of autos far more efficient, more economical, and, ultimately, more profitable. When you learn to eliminate your wasted therbligs, you, too, can learn to excel.

Another helpful tip is to learn some sort of shorthand. How many times have you tried to take important notes of a discussion and failed to get them all down because you were writing in longhand? In real estate you should take notes on everything: those potential clients that suggest interest in property, every good idea, every meeting, and certainly every negotiation. Date your notes, organize them, and file them. This will be an invaluable help in clearing up any misunderstandings. In addition, should you ever have to defend yourself or your interests in court, your notes will help to establish time, dates, and places of events and are permissible as proof of recollection.

I credit my own success less to intelligence and more to hard work and diligent use of my time. When I'm working, I make an effort not to waste a single minute of my time. Most people probably work from 8 a.m. to 5 p.m., five days a week, on average. But when I'm hard at work on a project, I'm up at 4 or 5 in the morning and working until 6 at night, six and sometimes seven days a week.

When you add up the hours, it's clear that I am putting in nearly two weeks' worth of hours where most competitors would only be putting in one. In essence, I've managed to do twice the work in the same time. That doesn't mean everybody has to follow the same pattern, but it shows the kind of dedication and investment of time I've pursued to get ahead in my career. I truly believe that I'll get out of work what I put into it.

My Typical Workday

In the morning I eat breakfast alone while I prepare a list of the day's objectives. Some of these activities might include:

- Call the owners/sellers of at least 10 expired listings.

- Call owners and other listing agents about vacant and buildable properties.

- Request surveys or plans of potential properties.

- Set various appointments to help achieve the day's objectives.

- Give multiple sales presentations to anyone who will listen.

- Check and respond to e-mails or telephone messages.

I spend the remainder of my morning and afternoon try-ing to complete all the objectives on my list. I try to follow up my e-mail or fax correspondence with a personal call to confirm the client received my information and ask if he or she has any questions.

To help stay organized, I also select certain days to per-form specific duties on a consistent basis. For example, on Mondays I'll prepare new marketing materials; on Tuesdays I'll preview new construction projects; on Wednesdays I pre-view available vacant properties; on Thursdays I preview new listings of others, and so on. I've found that discipline and consistency are other important keys to my success.

Once you've established good, consistent work habits, you'll find the road to success much smoother, with fewer surprises and obstacles in your way. (I'll discuss this fur-ther in Chapter 4.)

Obviously, the schedule I have described is intensive, and in order to work in this fashion, you have to love what you do. When you love your career, you'll feel that all of life is your playground. In the business of real estate, or anything else for that matter, I don't know many truly successful people who do not enjoy what they do.

The key word here is "successful." There are hundreds of real estate agents who don't like their job, and these people rarely achieve great success. Just about every suc-cessful agent I've come in contact with would tell you theirs is the best career they can imagine, and they wouldn't change jobs if they could.

This is very much true for me, too. If I had to repeat my life, I would have started in real estate much earlier!

My own motivation, my personal drive, was to learn the business that I was already involved in to some extent as an agent. I had to do it the hard way. When I started out in construction, I didn't go to school to learn how it all worked. I sat down with estimators to learn how to estimate plans. I sat down with draftsmen to learn how to draw floor plans. I made myself totally self-sufficient so that I would not have to depend on other people.

I know that I couldn't do my job nearly as well today if I didn't have a well-rounded education concerning every aspect of what I do. For a beginner starting out on a new project, it would probably take two months or so to put all of the pieces together. At this point, I could probably do it in two or three days, because I don't have to ask anybody. I have the knowledge of costs, construction, and legal issues, so I don't have to depend on anyone else.

As I mentioned, I've been employed as an aluminum siding salesman, a stockbroker, an investment banker, a builder, a real estate agent, a real estate broker, and I've always been a top producer in whatever I've done. I've achieved this not through superior intelligence, extraordinary skills, or great luck, but in large part through simple diligence and attitude. I get up in the morning with the idea that I'm eager, and every day's a new day; I already know what I am going to sell and who I want to sell it to. I get up every morning, even on weekends, with those same thoughts in mind. (I'm not thinking, "I don't want to go to work. I'm tired. I wonder what John's doing today? I'd rather go sailing.") I'm thinking about what I'm going to do today to better my business and place my family in a position where I will never have to worry about them, even after I'm gone.

Be Charitable: Doing Well by Doing Good

Ideally, I would like to be remembered as an honest, fair, and good man. Contrary to the stereotypes of many successful business types, I'm not a greedy person. I pay my agents more than any other agency in town, because I want them to walk out of the office with money; I want them to walk out of the office feeling that they and their families are secure. And I want to help them become successful. I spend every day trying to produce new products for them to sell, for them to make money. Presently, I can boast that almost all of the agents that have worked for my company for at least 18 months are paper millionaires.

Obviously, this means I'll make more money, too. I believe that when you let other people make money, it comes back to you in abundance.

Building Your Reputation

In real estate, as with any other business, establishing and maintaining allies is indispensable to your success. In the business world, your allies will protect your reputation and send you business as well. Your reputation, whether good or bad, will likely precede you wherever you go.

So I can't stress enough the importance of dealing with others in a forthright and aboveboard manner. I've come up with five basic covenants I believe will create the positive reputation that you'll need to be successful:

1. Always avoid negative statements about your peers.

2. Never go back on your word, even if it is severely to your detriment.

3. Always pay your debts in full and on time.

4. Always be on time for appointments. Being late is an insult to the person waiting, making it seem as if your time is more valuable than his.

5. Never leave another co-broker/agent thinking you didn't honor the commission amount you agreed upon.

These are simple and straightforward rules, but important to your business and personal success. You don't have to lie, cheat, or steal in order to become a multimillionaire.

In reality, the more integrity you have, the easier it is to grow your success. When you're seeking investments and you have a reputation of high integrity, your chances of success are much, much greater.

Maintaining Balance

This piece of advice may come as a surprise, but I think it's as important as anything else described here in maintaining a successful perspective. You've read all about patience and persistence involved in laying the groundwork for business success. Hard work and long hours are certainly a big part of this, but you must also remember to play!

That's right; recreation is the building block of life. Recreation not only releases the stress associated with your day-to-day work, it will improve your health and help keep your spouse and/or family more supportive of your efforts. Most people forget that the word "*recreation*" literally means "to re-create." You must re-create yourself continually so that you're positioned for success.

It may seem like a long road to achieving your dream at times, but there's no reason not to enjoy the journey.

Helping Others Achieve

How many times have you watched someone struggle to perform a task that's taking twice as long as it should? A word to the wise: Teach others to become more efficient. Share your knowledge, and mentor other bright people. You can't be truly great unless there are people around you doing great things.

Remember, your chain is only as strong as its weakest link. When you share your knowledge, help others to learn, give them confidence in themselves, and help them make money, you really have created a living, breathing, and walking billboard. This conveys to others around you that you're someone to be admired, and someone it pays to do business with.

Associate With the Right People

My next piece of advice may appear controversial, even a little bit harsh, but in my experience it's absolutely true. Success in business comes in large part through aligning yourself with the right kind of people, by which I mean people with integrity who can bring something to the table. This is true both in business and in your personal life.

After all, you've worked hard to educate yourself and to contribute to your community through your business and personal activities. Why shouldn't you demand the same of your colleagues? When you start paying attention to your associations, you'll find that dealing with people of integrity and similar dedication to their work ethic can do wonders for your prosperity. Your luck will simply seem to change, as new opportunities and deals come your way.

41

You've heard the saying before: "Tell me who your friends are and I'll tell you who you are." In the real estate business, this is certainly true.

Again, it may sound like simple advice, but here are some types to avoid:

- Anyone who cheats.

- Anyone who lies.

- Anyone who avoids paying his debts.

- Anyone who has unhealthy addictions.

- Anyone who cannot control her temper.

- Anyone who is unethical or suggests unethical actions.

Okay, we're through with the basics. Let's get started on your path to becoming a millionaire.

CHAPTER 3

NEGOTIATING THE WIN-WIN DEAL

We've all heard the term. But exactly what is a "win-win" deal?

A win-win deal is one in which everyone involved in the transaction benefits. It's essential in any real estate deal that both you and your opposing partner feel you've been treated fairly. The seller "wins" by receiving his or her asking price, or something close to it, for the unit. The purchaser "wins" by obtaining what he or she feels is the right property for the right price. Finally, the buyer of the completed project wins by receiving ownership in a sound and ultimately profitable real estate investment.

This transition of ownership describes the perfect win-win scenario. Everyone should feel that they got a great deal. As an agent, creating this kind of experience will breed referrals and help you turn a one-time customer into an ongoing client.

To negotiate a win-win deal, you must fully prepare yourself by planning ahead. As the real estate agent, you must lead your client into having only one simple, obvious, and logical conclusion: to make a purchase. You should always anticipate your client's thoughts, concerns, and responses, so that any potential objections can be overcome.

No matter what you're doing, whether buying, selling, or negotiating a new deal, your opponents should walk away thinking they have "won the joust." They should feel they've negotiated well and achieved the objective they wanted. Knowing in advance that all buyers and sellers ultimately want to win, my advice to you is let them do that. But let them win on your terms. I call this the art of letting someone have your way.

Using a Reference

Striking a real estate deal is, on one level, a straightforward legal transition of ownership; on another level, it's an elaborate interpersonal "dance" that may reflect each partner's closely held convictions, emotions, and a great deal of trust. For this reason, it's essential that both parties are comfortable going into a negotiation. The smallest sign of doubt or mistrust by either side can trip things up and threaten to capsize the deal.

That's why it can be extremely helpful to have a third-party reference prior to going into a negotiation. When someone reputable can vouch for your integrity, achievements, and good intentions, the opposing side will be that much more at ease. Ideally, you would use someone known to both parties involved in the transaction, or at least a reference whose objectivity can be assured.

No matter what your financial assets are, if you have a credible person recommend you, you share the benefit of his or her credibility. You have to start out by getting credible people to believe in you. You have to build your reputation by always doing what you say you're going to do, when you say you're going to do it, and by always protecting your investor to the very end, even if you don't make any money yourself. You have to protect his or her investment first and know that yours will come second, sometimes last, or maybe not at all!

Even though most of my contracts protect me from direct liability, and I don't have collateral behind them, I don't allow other people to lose money in my dealings. Even when I'm not technically required to repay them, I do.

The bigger your vision, the more important it becomes to have a qualified, in-person reference. Obviously, you can't just send a letter out to a potential investor blindly and ask them to make a million-dollar investment. You have to have someone introduce you to that person personally. You might want to start asking around among your friends, because the odds are somebody you know knows somebody else who has money. That's where you have to start. Ask your friend to introduce you to that potential investor, and bear in mind that he or she will likely have other friends with money.

Having a promising list of referrals won't negate the need for doing your homework. In fact, here it becomes even more critical. You should always come to potential investors with a thorough and well thought-out presentation. If they can't make an investment themselves, they may recommend you to somebody else if you have made a good enough impression.

Bear in mind that you have to be cautious and be sure you're adhering to securities law and dealing only with qualified investors. This usually means a single person who makes $250,000 or more, a married couple making $300,000 or more, or anyone with a net worth of a million dollars or more. Common sense tells you that if you're dealing with investors of high net worth, you won't be as exposed as if you were dealing with someone's last dollar. You never want to risk somebody's nest egg. When in doubt, it's best to consult with an attorney with some expertise in investments and securities law.

Advice on Reaching a Deal

Earlier in this chapter I talked about letting your opponent "win" when you make a deal. To help ensure his or her final satisfaction, you should be careful not to move things too quickly or make reaching a bargain seem too easy. Inevitably, human nature will affect every business transaction. No matter what the final price is, it's natural for the buyer or seller to wonder whether he's gotten a "deal."

Think about it. If you're in a negotiation process, and your opposing side gives in right away, you're going to wonder if you could have pressed them for more or less, depending on which side you're on. This is what's commonly known as buyer's or seller's remorse.

In a worst-case scenario, this reaction can result in a client wanting to back out of the deal, or to renegotiate the price and terms of the contract. Bearing this in mind, you should always go into a sale with the expectation that you're going to have to negotiate extensively, down to the last dollar of the difference between the two parties, regardless of how simple the deal may appear.

My advice is to always make your first offer a little less than what you know your seller will want to accept. This gives you some movement in negotiating the terms and price. Be careful not to offer something too far below the mark, though, because your seller is likely to counter demand an amount that's at or very near her final asking price, which effectively shuts down your negotiation.

Also, if an initial offer is far too low, it čan easily be construed as insulting and break up the deal then and there.

For example, let's say a buyer made an offer to you, the seller, to purchase your home. You have been shown a competitive market analysis (CMA) and agree with the CMA report that your property is worth approximately $200,000 on the current market. If the buyer offers you $100,000, you're not going to take his offer seriously and may in fact refuse to negotiate any further.

But if I, as the buyer, had offered you $180,000, and you were truly motivated to sell your property, you would probably come back with a counteroffer in the neighborhood of $190,000, leaving room for more practical, amicable negotiations.

In my dealings, I have found these words insightful: You don't make people buy or sell; you make them *want* to buy or sell.

Contracts

Okay, we have established that a win-win deal means that everyone involved gains something of value to him or her. Because every real estate transaction involves drafting a contract, let's talk a bit about contracts, a crucial element in any real estate deal.

While most people, understandably, become fixated on the price of a property in a transaction, I've found that negotiating desirable terms on your contract is often more important than getting a lower purchase price, as long as the price allows for a reasonable profit margin for the end product after closing.

In a real estate purchase, the contract must include terms that allow potential customers time to perform their due diligence (also known as a "feasibility study" or "research period"). This lets the buyer verify the facts given at the time of the contract and investigate any unknown factors that might affect the use of the property.

The feasibility study or due diligence period gives a buyer time to ensure that his or her intended use for the property is allowable, and that there is indeed a market for its use and a resulting profit from it.

The best deals I've made in my real estate career have required minimal "at risk" deposits up front or during the due diligence period. I generally require that my deposits be refundable during the due diligence period. You should always be wary of deals that require a large amount of cash up front. (In most cases you won't have the amount of cash you would need available right away, so you would use the due diligence period to attract other investors and to bring the deal together with limited cash and risk on your own part.)

49

I always insist on a reasonable due diligence period as a term of any contract I sign. That reasonable time depends on the property's intended use. On a condominium project, for example, I consider three to six months a reasonable amount of time can (see Option to Purchase contract sample on page 163).

Once I've had a free, six-month look at the property, with a small refundable deposit from me or my investors, I will then make a larger, nonrefundable deposit that would extend the due diligence period for an additional 12 or more months. I usually offer to make substantial nonrefundable monthly payments that apply to the purchase price. This assures the seller that you are sincere about closing on the property. For large condominium projects, these extensions are necessary, because most condo projects take a great deal of time to reach the construction loan phase, which is usually when I pay off the land.

Note: When drawing up this type of contract, be sure to state that all your deposits will apply to the original purchase price. This type of option contract allows the necessary time to investigate the deal with minimal risk to the investor. It also gives the landowner some level of comfort, knowing that if you don't ultimately close on the deal, he or she has at least received payment for the time the property was taken off the market.

Consider this: If you were to buy a $10-million piece of land and make interest payments on it for up to two and a half years, while waiting on the construction loan to close, your costs would be substantial. However, my blueprint involves agreeing to what may be a slightly higher purchase price in order to get the contract terms you need with no interest payments. This way, whatever payments you make will be applied to the final purchase price with ultimately a lower cost of purchase.

The 1031 Exchange

If you're advising a potential seller, having this vital piece of information can help overcome one of the most common obstacles to making a deal.

The 1031 Exchange is an excellent alternative for those who want to sell their rental property, but fear the resulting taxes would be unbearable and that after they've been paid, there won't be enough cash left to buy a new property. Named for Internal Revenue Code(I.R.C.) Section 1031, a 1031 Exchange allows a seller to defer taxes on the profit he or she makes when selling investment real estate. In exchange, it requires the seller to comply with a few basic requirements:

1. The properties being bought and sold must be of like kind.

2. Seller has 45 days from the date of closing on the old property to identify up to three

new properties that he or she is considering for purchase.

3. Seller has 180 days from the date of closing to close the purchase of one of these properties under consideration.

4. By law, the money received from the sale of the first property must be held by a   . "Qualified Intermediary."

5. The titleholder of the old property has to remain the titleholder of the new property. The seller cannot touch the money received from the sale.

6. Because the seller's aim is to avoid any taxable gain, he/she must reinvest all cash proceeds and buy a suitable property of equal or greater value.

Summary for Achieving the Win-Win Deal

Here is the skinny on the win-win theme:

- Think ahead. Before entering into any negotiation, you should have a clear idea of the most you will pay or give up.

- Analyze and anticipate your opponent's motivations and objectives, so you understand where he or she is coming from, and what aspects or elements of a deal might affect his or her decisions.

- Make your initial offer a little less than the amount that you're willing to pay and a bit lower than you think the other side will accept.

Ultimately, you want to give the opposite party what he wants (purchase price) in exchange for what you want (favorable contract terms). That's how everybody wins.

CHAPTER 4

LEVERAGING YOUR SUCCESS

In real estate, as in all professions, being known for your successes is a badge of honor. Therefore, I take great pride in who I am and what I am known as: a dealmaker. I've said before that some people are naturally born salespeople, while others have acquired the skills through learning and over time. But even those who are natural-born salespeople must work hard to build a base of knowledge on the product that they're selling.

"You won't see it until you believe it."

Read this quote again and think about it.

It's my belief, after years spent working across a variety of career fields, that no matter what your interest, you should go into any endeavor with the certainty that you are going to succeed. As a salesperson, I live by the rule that there is no room for negative comments or negative thoughts in your life! I learned that negative thoughts spread like a cancer. I have learned not to think negative thoughts, nor do i allow negativity from others in my presence.

When you encourage and exude positive thinking, others will pick up on your positive attitude. Such an attitude results in confidence, admiration, and success over time. I believe that excitement is contagious, in any form, and that excitement can cause a person to exceed his or her abilities.

I've also learned that success breeds success; success grows exponentially. Once you have completed a successful project and it becomes known throughout your community, you'll find that people bring you new projects at an increasing rate. With each new success, your confidence and reputation are bolstered. The result is that more influential people will know you and more salespeople will want to sell for you.

Show Business: Market Yourself for Success

In order to succeed in a big way, you have to view what you're doing as a form of show business. In other words, you have to put yourself out in the public's eye in a big way. One way to do this is to write stories for the local newspaper or trade magazine, and to try to get coverage for yourself when you've accomplished something exceptional and of interest.

Understand that newspapers love press releases and use them freely. It's a great way to advertise yourself with few out-of-pocket expenses. If you're part of a real estate company, have the company actively tout your successes: Every time you have a successful sales month, you should send a press release to the local newspaper. Other potentially newsworthy stories include naming the top salesperson or listing agent within your area.

Even though your activity may seem routine to you, creating some "buzz" through a newspaper or magazine story helps to generate excitement. Getting your name out there helps create an image of you that people will remember. Aggressive and successful people tend to gravitate toward others who are successful and famous: Success breeds success!

Your Website is another important tool for communicating your image as a reputable, respected professional. Some people take the shortcut of a do-it-yourself software program, but the results look decidedly homemade. Take my advice and hire a talented Web firm to create a first-class site for you. It's cheaper than you may think. And remember that it will be on display all the time, for all to see.

Be Memorable

When I was first getting into the real estate business, I met a guy from Chicago who seemed to be quite successful, although I knew that he had only recently received his real estate license. I asked him how he was achieving such success, and he told me that immediately after getting his license he went out and rented a Superman outfit, called the local newspaper, and told them that he was going to climb on top of a building dressed as the comic book hero. Sure enough, a few reporters showed up to cover this "news" story, at which time he took the opportunity to pronounce to the public that he was the greatest real estate salesman in the world. (And after tracking his career, I think he has almost accomplished it!)

True, his idea is extreme, but often it's this kind of innovative and unconventional thinking that can jump-start a career. The key is to think of the press as your ally, and use them as much as you can.

Success Favors the Bold

Modesty is an admirable quality in personal life, but in this business you can't shy away from letting others know about your successes. Everybody likes to deal with a winner, one who helps other people make money. In order to be a winner, you have to be aggressive.

As you succeed in different areas, people start paying attention and talking about you to their friends. ("Did you know Jerry went out and sold a million-dollar piece of property, and the next week he sold a $2 million piece of property as well?" Or even better: "I want to do a deal with him!" Or "Did you know Jerry has put together a project that's going to be worth around $50 million?") Over time, these kinds of comments add a great deal to your credibility, and ultimately people will want to do business with you based on your credibility, not because of your dreams.

One major attraction to the real estate industry is that there's little in the way of hierarchy; in many ways, the playing field here is wide open. Your success is really based on astute planning and execution, creating a viable concept, making good decisions, negotiating good deals, having a reputation for honesty, and so on.

The way you capture someone's attention is not necessarily telling her the length of tenure and resume, but by finding the right property, putting the right deal together, and showing investors how much money they can actually make. Do this, and you have their attention. What's more, you have a sweet deal.

You don't have to be an expert with years of experience as long as your figures are honest, the pro forma is accurate, and you're giving prospective customers the right information.

Think Big

"Ah but a man's reach should exceed his grasp...."

—Robert Browning

Personally, I'm not interested in selling a home or condominium that someone intends to use as a primary residence. Experience has taught me that I'm better off focusing on real estate investors, for example, someone who may purchase multiple units at one time instead of only one.

I'd much rather sell five units to one person as an investment, because I get my project sold out faster, I earn more commission, and it's much easier for me to do. I could sell five condos over the telephone in far less time than it would take to sell someone a condo to live in. Because, in that situation, I have to go show it to them in person, and I might spend two weeks showing them various condos before they decide to buy, if they do decide to buy. If not, I've wasted all that time, gas, and effort for nothing.

In my opinion, preconstruction condominium sales offer the real blueprint for making money. Preconstruction sales are sales made prior to the completion and/or delivery of a real estate property.

Most people who start projects make the mistake of starting out too small. Conventional wisdom is to start small and grow, but my advice is just the opposite: Think big! It usually takes as much time to put a small deal together as it does a big deal, and if there's more money for you in the big deal, why not go for it? My first project was $160 million! Had I ever done something like that before? Never! Did I think I could pull it off? Absolutely!

I have learned through the years that if you don't think big, you'll never be big. And if you don't believe that you can do something, then you probably can't. You must possess the full belief that you can achieve your goal, even if you don't have all the direct knowledge of how to do it yourself. You have to believe that once you get things to a point where you can show other people its potential for profit, they'll agree to bring their money and talents to the table and offer their help.

In my own case, no sooner had I started the ball rolling on the $160 million project, that I immediately began planning a $220 million and a $350 million project as well. For my very first project, I started by putting down my own small savings and my wife looked at me like I was crazy.

"Where are you going to get the money to do that?" she asked, and I told her not to worry, that it would come. Sure enough, it did!

When I started the next project, she asked the same question, and my response was the same. For my most recent project, the one estimated at around $350 million, she continued to ask "Where are you going to get the money?" and I continued to assure her that the money would come!

Presently, my projects are valued in excess of $3 billion. This was accomplished in approximately three and a half years.

What I'm trying to say is that when you set your mind to accomplish a project, and you believe in yourself enough, you really can do it. Follow the precepts of my blueprint and you can carry it through!

Blueprint for Leveraging Success

- Be confident and proud of your deal-making status.

- Learn your product.

- Proceed positively; believe that what you're presenting is viable.

- Publicize, publicize, publicize.

- Think big; go after the bigger deals that are both easier and more profitable.

- Seek relationships with those who would lend their credibility to you.

"Whatever you truly believe you are, you are!"

Successful real estate entrepreneurs understand that you must establish yourself as a recognized and reputable real estate professional. From here you will begin to truly leverage your success. In the simplest terms, your reputation will create confidence in you with your peers. This confidence will catch the attention of bigger and bigger investors or partners.

You need to think of yourself, and market yourself, as an attraction. Ever heard of a man named Donald Trump? That's how you leverage success.

CHAPTER 5

THE BEGINNING

How I Got Started

As I've said, Florida was the jumping-off point for me as a real estate agent/developer and remains my primary market today. Majestic Beach Towers, in Panama City Beach, Florida, was the first property I developed using my own money with no outside developers involved. Although I'd accumulated a great deal of knowledge about the industry, having worked for some time as a real estate agent, I realized that I really wasn't using all this knowledge to my best advantage. I knew I needed to find an avenue through which to direct it toward helping me reach my full potential.

So I had an epiphany of sorts. I sat down one day and asked myself, "Why am I using all my knowledge to help other people and developers make money? Why not help myself?"

My own decision was based on what I saw as multifold possibilities. I knew I wanted to sell preconstruction water-front condominiums. With the list of investors I compiled, I had the ability to notify each one of them promptly and get these properties under contract in a very short amount of time. My investors would then have the opportunity to purchase several units at once. They would also have the luxury to choose from many different-sized condominium units available to them.

Another important factor in my decision was the knowledge that the price trend in condos was escalating upward with increasing momentum. These units were expensive, which meant I had the potential to earn huge commissions!

I decided to do some more field work. In September of 2001, I drove to Panama City Beach, Florida, to investigate condominium properties. In less than two hours I had spotted the Majestic Motel, dilapidated but still operating, with approximately 450 feet of beach front. I called immediately, spoke to the owners, and made arrangements to meet them.

Things progressed rather quickly. After some back-and-forth negotiations, in October 2001 I obtained my very own

Gulf-front land contract. Because I never think small, I immediately began talking with neighbors on both sides and across the street. A few days and months later, I'd received another contract for more Gulf-front property, followed by four other contiguous purchase contracts, giving me 650 feet of Gulf front and enough property across the street for parking. My project, Majestic Beach Towers, was still in the planning stages and had been largely pre-sold within six months, at which time I made a deal to sell 80 percent of the ownership to an experienced developer with the money I did not have to complete the project.

I didn't sell ownership percentage for the money; my goal was to acquire the means to get my project completed and free myself to seek out another project. With percentage sale accomplished, I started acquiring land for my next undertaking, Shores of Panama in Panama City Beach, Florida, only a few thousand yards down the beach. My first of four land contracts required was made in June 2002.

Again, I proceeded to pre-sell the new project as I put it together. When I had sufficient sales and the necessary land secured, I found another experienced and well-heeled developer and sold him 80 percent. Meanwhile, I began working to secure a third project, known as Laketown Wharf. The target property was actually directly across the street from Shores of Panama, consisting of about five acres situated on a pristine 16-acre lake. The first of 12 parcels was contracted in October of 2003. This time I did not need to sell any of the interest out; I'd gone from much less than one half-million dollars' net worth to a projected net worth of more than $100 million in only two years. Presently, I have seven additional major projects in development (and mostly sold out), which has increased my projected net worth to more than $250 million in only three and one half years. In addition to those that are in development, I have numerous other projects that are in the planning stage, pushing the approximate collective sell-out values to more than $3 billion.

Prior to my actual ownership of these developments, I helped bring about several projects in my area for other developers:

- Emerald Towers West, Okaloosa Island, Florida.

- Island Princess, Okaloosa Island, Florida.

- Destin West, Okaloosa Island, Florida.

Financing

Obtaining full financing for my initial projects would have been a major problem had I not passed off the 80 percent on the first two projects to other, better-funded developers. I reserved the balance of 20 percent ownership knowing that the developers would eventually offer to buy it all. Since that time, I've had no problems with financing and have financed my newer projects with 100 percent ownership and no financial help.

My bankers and peers recently asked how I managed to dramatically increase my net worth to several hundred million in a mere three and one half years. In summation of this question: First I located the property that I wished to develop, and wrote an option to purchase that property with a $10,000 refundable deposit, which was a lot of money for me at the time. When writing the option, I stipulated that I receive 50 percent of the sales commission because I was a licensed real estate agent and was also the procuring cause for the sale. In fact, I increased the amount of the purchase price by the extra amount of commission I wanted to receive for the real estate work when the construction loan was eventually issued. I told the seller what I was doing and required that he pay this extra commission to my brokerage company. This little secret increases your net worth substantially, while giving you the cash flow to move onto your next project.

The option was written to allow me six months for due diligence and 30 months to close; therefore, I was at virtually no risk during those first six months. With the first option in hand, I proceeded to secure additional options on the adjacent properties with the same terms, but smaller deposit amounts.

My next step was to create a proposed site plan for the project and a matching proforma identifying the cost and expected profit for the project. Immediately after completing an acceptable pro forma and obtaining a project layout with tentative floor plans, I set the unit prices and began to pre-sell the units. Once having a good number of pre-sales (reservations), I started the architect on the serious drawing and started the financing process.

CHAPTER 6

INSIGHTS

I don't sell any product to anyone

that I would not buy myself!

Finding Resources

When you're new to the real estate development business, getting a grip on price and the value of real estate property can seem daunting, especially because there are so many variables involved. Fortunately, there are resources available to help you determine the amount you can expect to pay and earn for a property or on a project. Some of these local resources are real estate agents, cost estimators at building supply companies, architects, and appraisers. There are guide lines for apartments versus office buildings; some estimate

value per square foot, and others per unit. Some of these guidelines can be found in your local library in construction estimating books, software programs, and by contacting local builders of such projects.

In pricing resort condominium projects, people used to go by square foot or by acres, and as property became more valuable, people started looking at values per front foot. As it grew even more valuable, and people recognized that different square footages can be different depths, people shifted to using a per unit cost. My feeling is that what you pay for a property is less important than making sure your overall project works, meaning all the parties involved walk away satisfied and you earn a reasonable amount on your initial investment.

I frequently find developers trying to beat property owners down on their prices, but often they fail to get their proposed project in place because they've been so focused on how much the landowner is going to make. I look at things differently; I do want the landowner to make money and to feel like he got a good deal, because that way I can get the terms that I need.

As I said before, terms are more critical than cost when you're developing condominiums. You want the numbers to work, as long as you can demonstrate the ability to earn a profit, which is what the bank will require before it will give you a loan.

II

THE BLUEPRINT

CHAPTER 7

THE BLUEPRINT

Napoleon Bonaparte once said, "For everything there must be a plan." Another noted philosopher, Yogi Berra, added his two cents: "If you don't know where you're going, you could wind up somewhere else." Real estate investors need to plan, too.

Let's face it: Anytime you start a new project, whether it's a procurement of listings, assemblage of properties, pre-planning of a planned unit development, a condo development, or any other type of real estate deal, you need to do it in an organized way. I usually start with a three-ring binder, where all the original information about a particular project is kept for my records and future use. This is what I refer to as the "documentation." I would also advise you to scan every document or note into a digital document file, such as PaperPort, in your computer. This allows for easy location, access, and transfer to others.

The document book primarily helps you organize and outline the most important details of your project prior to soliciting bids, making a sales pitch, or applying for a loan. The better prepared you are with details, numbers, and hard data to support your pitch, the better your chances for success.

The second book that will be required is called the "project overview" book. It should contain the following information:

- Renderings.

- Drawings.

- Site plans.

- Site layouts.

- Elevations.

- Schematics.

- Amenities.

- Proposed prices.

- Square footage.

- Location.

- Nearby attractions.

- Floor plans.

- Aerial photos.

- Marketing plan.

- Sales personnel.

Land Buying Guide

Before you actually set about implementing your project, it's important to clear up any questions and know exactly what you're going after and/or getting. The following are common questions you should carefully consider prior to any real estate or land purchase.

- Is the location appropriate for your envisioned project?

- What's the land price?

- Does the owner own it free and clear? If not, how much is owed? (Having this knowledge will help you structure your offer.)

- Are there easements or leases on the property that will affect your use?

- Where are the easements to the property?

- Is there title insurance on this property? With whom?

Title insurance insures the lender and optionally the new owner from any future claims against the title to a property. In the event of a claim, the insurance company will fight and/or settle the claim for either or both the lender and/or owner.

There are various types of easements on a parcel of land; most have to do with utilities and services that don't normally affect the value or use of the property. Some easements, such as pedestrian and vehicular easements, do affect the property's value and use. That's why it's important to find out which kind apply in your case.

Are there covenants, codes, and/or deed restrictions (CCRs) on the property?

When a parcel of land has been subdivided, there are usually covenants, codes, and restrictions placed on the property to protect the individual owners from one another.

These covenants, codes, and restrictions (or CCRs) are recorded with the subdivision and apply to the title of a property for a period of up to 30 years.

What type of deed will I be getting?

There are numerous types of deeds, but the most common one is a warranty deed. The warranty deed is the most protective kind, one in which the seller warrants free and clear title to the buyer and stands ready to defend that title for the buyer.

What is the current zoning?

Because zoning regulations govern how the land may be used, they obviously have a strong influence on land sales. For example, land with commercial zoning may sell for 10 or 20 times as much as land zoned for agriculture. So before you purchase the property, make sure you understand the zoning. Find out if your land can be subdivided. Are there environmental restrictions? What kinds of structures are permitted?

If rezoning will be required for your particular type of development, have the seller sign a Change of Zoning Request authorization letter. This will save you a lot of time.

Zoning maps are usually kept at the county courthouse or other government agency responsible for land-use planning in your area. If you don't feel comfortable researching this on your own, you might choose to get help from a property appraiser or real estate agent.

What are the permitted and non-permitted uses?

A city or county normally has a planning and zoning department that controls the land uses within its boundaries. For example, a city will establish a comprehensive plan for the entire area within the city limits. This plan identifies in different colors and with different zoning codes for the type of activity—commerce, residence, manufacturing, recreation, and so on—that is or is not allowed in each area.

What types of structures are permitted on this land?

This is generally determined by the allowed uses in the specific zone where you property is located.

What is the allowed density?

The allowed residential density on property determines the number of units that can be legally placed on the property. This will also influence the profitability of your project.

Is there a height restriction?

This can also influence the number of living units and therefore your profitability.

Can the parcel of property be subdivided?

The zoning code will tell you whether your land can be subdivided. If the rules say it can't, you might be able to apply for a variance, which is basically an exception, although these can sometimes be hard to obtain.

Are there access considerations?

In other words, is there deeded beach access if it's on the coast, or is there access to contiguous or nearby natural attractions?

Is it landlocked?

Are there other land parcels, not owned by you, that might block access to public roads, beaches, and so on? Note that by law, very few states will allow a piece of land to be sold without direct access to public roads.

What utilities and other municipal services (power, sewer, water) are readily available?

The current owner, or the local utility company, should be able to tell you.

Is there a survey or map available? Any renderings or drawings?

Aerial maps can be found at city or county appraiser's offices; other sources include a local surveyor's office, which may have performed an earlier survey on the property. An architect can supply you with drawings if they haven't already been made.

Is the property in a flood zone? If yes, which flood zone?

Any local insurance company that offers flood insurance would be a good place to find this out.

What, if any, additional rules and regulations apply?

If the property or subdivision is controlled by a homeowner's association, it should provide you with any additional rules.

What a Seller Should Know

When you sell land, try to keep in mind the buyer's motivations. For example, if you're selling a waterfront lot in a new subdivision, you might appeal to potential buyers by showing off the swimming or boating opportunities. If you're selling a country lot with a view of the mountains, explain why it's the perfect spot to build a vacation getaway. Simply put, you want to make it easy for a buyer to visualize his or her future plans taking shape on your property.

Setting the Right Selling or Purchase Price

Unless you're very familiar with land sales in your area, most real estate experts recommend working with an appraiser or real estate agent to arrive at a proper asking or offering price. Appraisers work for a set fee, and will research recent sales of comparable properties to determine market value. If you decide to work with an agent, try to find someone who specializes in land sales, or whatever applies to your project, if it isn't land. Make sure to read the listing contract and understand how the land will be marketed and the amount of the commission.

For your own education, it's a good idea to keep a close eye on listings in the local newspapers, as well as reading the real estate and business news, for updates on zoning changes, new developments from various neighborhoods, and any other trends that might affect property values in your area.

Municipal Services

When you invest in real estate, think utilities. Generally speaking, your property will be more attractive to buyers if it includes easy access to municipal services, such as power, water, and sewer. This isn't a problem for most subdivision lots where services are already in place, but in some rural areas, just having a well on the property can drastically increase its value. So don't hesitate to let buyers know about any improvements that have been made on a property.

Selling Subdivision Lots

When you sell a lot in a subdivision or a unit in a condominium project, remember that you're selling the development and community as much as the land. Buyers will be particularly interested to know what sort of community or project amenities exist, such as parks, schools, retail shopping, entertainment, and pools, and the types of homes or condos that have already been built in the area. Other important factors are the CCRs (covenants, codes, and restrictions), which can cover everything from the types and sizes of homes that can be built there to what color fences are allowed in backyards. Condominium owners are usually restricted from changing the exterior appearance of the unit and building. Homeowner restrictions are often a positive selling point because they ensure the development will have a certain degree of consistency, and therefore a stabilizing effect on property values.

Seeing Is Believing

Visuals count. Real estate consumers love to see pictures of property, floor plans, amenities, and exterior renderings.

The more you can offer, the better. These days, with Internet and digital technology, there's no reason you can't provide plenty of quality images; frankly, you're at a huge disadvantage if you don't. Your Website, brochures, and advertisements should include pictures of the land and any improvements. If there's a marvelous view from the property, show it off! And if you're advertising the property online, buyers appreciate having links to maps, local Websites, and any other information that helps showcase the location.

The Closing

"Closing" is the term for the final step in the real estate transaction, when money actually changes hands, title is transferred, and all the final documents are signed. If you're working with a real estate agent, he'll be able to make arrangements for all the paperwork. If you're selling land on your own, most title companies will handle the closing for a fee, or in some cases free of charge if they're writing a new title insurance policy for the property.

Price

If you're just starting out, you'll have to do some research to find the probable land value of the parcel you are considering. Initially, in the absence of an appraisal of the property, you'll want to find comparisons, sometimes called "comps," of other similar land in the area of the parcel of interest. Comps can be acquired through your local Multiple Listing Services (MLS); if you're not presently a real estate agent, you can get help from a real estate agent who has an MLS membership to look up recent sales and listings of similar properties.

With time and experience, you'll get a feel for the real values of different properties in your area. The better you know your region, the better equipped you'll be to make quick decisions on whether to buy or sell a piece of property. Time is of the essence when you're looking at desirable areas; therefore, the sooner you can learn the values of land in your area, the closer you'll be to getting the right parcels at the right time.

Utilities

You need to contact the various utility services providers for your property location to determine the availability of each type of service (telephone, power, water, sewer, garbage, and so on).

Other

Drawings, also called renderings, can be made by a local architect once you have determined what you think you want to build on the property. Try to get the architect and civil engineer to reduce the front-end charges, leaving the larger balances due upon the issue of the construction loan.

Homeowner's Associations

You'll find that it's standard for subdivisions and condominium projects to have a homeowner's association, which essentially governs the appearance of properties within the same area and may also set regulations on permitted activities, lawn or garden maintenance, and so on. A developer of either type of project is usually responsible for setting up an association that would later be turned over to the homeowners.

What Do Land Buyers Look For?

Because land is a commodity that very rarely loses value, it's a wonderful way for investors to make a profit without incurring much risk. Regardless of whether your clients are looking for long- or short-term investments, you should be prepared for some common buyer questions about the housing market, area stability, economic base of the community, building costs, and anything else that you think would make a buyer feel at ease purchasing land in your community.

CHAPTER 8

WHAT TO DO TOMORROW

Interview With Jerry Wallace, the "Dealmaker"

The following is an interview with yours truly on the typical "day in the life" of a real estate entrepreneur. I'm including it here because it provides a good blueprint of what life is like in the real estate investment world.

Give us an example of your typical day. Do you need to meet a daily sales quota?

I don't feel the need to meet a specific sales quota but I do have a goal every day, and that is to produce as much as

I possibly can with my time. I have trained myself to get up every morning thinking of the day as a race that I have to go out and win.

What's a typical schedule for you?

4–5 a.m.: I read the mail over breakfast, along with the local real estate and business news. I also create a to-do list for the day with tasks I want to accomplish in order of priority.

6 a.m.: Go to my office and pay the bills.

6:30 a.m.: Start to tackle my to-do list, which normally includes writing or rewriting contracts, pro formas, listings, and so on.

7:30 a.m.: The telephone starts to ring, and the workday begins in earnest. Much of my day is taken up on the telephone, talking to investors, advertisers, purchasers, agents, and others.

6 p.m.: Go home, eat dinner, and spend time with my family.

7:30 p.m.: Go to bed.

This is a typical schedule for me, seven days a week, except for those times when I feel physically or mentally burned out. At times like that, I'll go for a motorcycle ride, or go fishing or power boating to blow off steam and clear my head.

Most models for successful real estate executives require the hiring of a large staff. Do you train assistants to manage your business?

Until recently I had no assistants, other than someone to answer the phone and help keep the books.

Do you develop your own marketing materials?

Yes, I design my own marketing material, often using Microsoft's Publisher software. For newspaper ads I usually hand draw what I want, then give it to the newspaper staff to lay out. I rarely hire an outside company to do my marketing or publishing.

How do you develop leads for preconstruction properties?

The very best lead for this type property is someone who already owns this kind of property, and therefore has experienced the great monetary returns that are possible through their purchase and resale. Local tax records will list all the owners of condominiums in your area and are a good source for those names and addresses. I usually hire a listing company that already has access to those lists, and I have it print up the material that I put together. The marketing company will also handle the mailings, for a fee.

What kinds of media do you find best for marketing?

My primary advertising vehicles are direct mail, television infomercials, television real estate shows, local newspapers, golf course publications, and real estate advertising books.

How do you track your leads?

We have all calls directed to one person who's assigned to handle leads and ask the callers where they got our name. We also have a toll-free number for people to call from our infomercials. The people at the toll-free number keep track of those calls for me.

Do you personally call leads back?

I used to, until I got so busy that I couldn't do it myself anymore. Now I refer all of my personal leads to my licensed real estate agents.

How do you sell property that hasn't been built yet?

With this kind of property, you're really selling the "sizzle" and not the steak. I've designed a clear, attractive, one-page presentation showing property appreciation in the area for this type property during the last 11 years and the potential return to those who want to buy and resell their property based on other similar properties. I'm not selling the individual unit so much as the entire project and its amenities. I do not promise anyone that he will make even one dime of profit. If you make promises, those promises are not only illegal, but will come back to haunt you.

Do you have a full-time staff?

I do own a real estate company and I defer all of the real estate questions to the broker of record, which isn't me. On the development side, I've learned enough to put most deals together without other staff. But I do have a staff that works with me on the show business side of my businesses. I presently have numerous different companies that I either run or help run.

How do you convert cold calls to appointments?

To save time, I try not to make in-person appointments with potential buyers of condominium units because I can usually sell to them over the telephone. I find I have enough people calling me for appointments, so I normally don't have to approach them myself. One exception is that occasionally I will sell a few condos while I eat breakfast at the local Waffle House or when I am at the beach with my boat *Dealmaker*.

What about handling your out-of-state customers?

I handle mostly everything I do on the telephone. The only time I deal with a client face to face is when I'm negotiating property purchases that I want to make for a particular project.

What do you wear when meeting with clients?

I try to model myself on Sam Walton in this regard, which means I wear what's comfortable for me. I'm not trying to impress anyone with my wardrobe, but with my thoughts and real estate concepts. Blue jeans, a polo shirt, and no socks are my typical summer attire; although for TV appearances I may have to dress more formally. Occasionally, when I am going to a meeting to negotiate a large land purchase, I will have my chauffeur drive me in a black limousine for a good first impression for making the landowner feel more comfortable about whether I can afford his property.

How did you gain confidence when you were just starting out?

Confidence comes from having both knowledge and sincerity, and I believe that these qualities are within the grasp of any new agent who really wants to pursue them.

Real estate guidebooks often advise using preprinted scripts when calling potential customers. Do you use scripts when calling people?

I have never used preprinted scripts in selling, because I don't want to sound like I have a "canned" pitch. If you have enough knowledge of your product, you'll never need a script to make a sale.

How many customers do you contact in a day?

I used to contact hundreds of people in a single day, but now I've honed my sales skills to the point where I can make the same amount of sales with far fewer contacts. That's the advantage of selling multiple units to a single buyer and why I'd recommend it to anyone else starting out. Never think *one* of any investment you are selling. If one is good, then two or more are better!

Do you teach agents to sell your way?

Yes, I present sales seminars to train my agents how to sell preconstruction, or to sell anything, for that matter. I have now trained others who can also lead these seminars.

What is your definition of success?

My definition of success is to be able to live comfortably with my family, to relax and enjoy what I've earned, and to have enough cash in the bank so I don't have to worry about paying bills. I would like to feel confident that I am a person whom others respect, and that I have completed or am moving toward God's mission for me. Finally, I want to know that I got where I am by ethical and moral means so that I can feel good about myself in every way.

CHAPTER 9

THE AFFILIATE PROGRAM

Most real estate brokers and companies that have exclusive right of sale listings with developers of subdivisions or condominiums do not want to share their sales opportunities with outside agents and brokers. One simple reason is they make more money on each sale by selling the units in-house. This attitude is not good for the developer (seller) because the sales may go much slower than if numerous companies and agents are advertising and selling.

I created what is called an affiliate program. Under this program my agents are encouraged to enroll outside companies and agents locally and nationally to sell units through them and receive an override on all sales made by those affiliates. This program has tripled and quadrupled the total number of sales and the amount of commissions credited to each of my agents on each project. My real estate company, Prestige Resort Properties, LLC, has hundreds of affiliates all over the country. This program allows companies with a limited number of agents to exceed the sales of companies 10 to 20 times our size. The large volume of sales also brings other developers needing sales to our company.

This program and the use of the Internet helps our affiliate agents anywhere in the country participate in the hot markets where I develop by giving them immediate access to updated inventory availability and pricing of units.

Note: This is intended for reference only and is not an approved program.

The following information and programs may be purchased through Jerry Wallace Companies. For prices and service please contact info@jerrywallacecompanies.com.

- Newsletter Subscription (Purchase)

- Training CD (Purchase for personal use)

- 30-minute Customized Infomercial CD (Purchase resale)

- Customized Infomercial for citywide broadcast (Purchase)

- Affiliate Website (Purchase)

Agent Sales Compensation Plan

We pay referral fees and/or commissions that far exceed most compensation offered in our area and maybe in your area. If you are interested in getting information regarding the affiliate program or about present properties being offered by Jerry Wallace Companies, call Prestige Resort Properties at 888-301-9899 or go to the Website *www.prestigeresortproperties.com.*

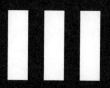

POWER
BROKERING

CHAPTER 10

EVALUATING YOUR CHANCES FOR SUCCESS

After you've done your homework and carefully considered the possibilities, you will have found the market in which you want to specialize. You know what you want to sell and to whom. Now that you have that knowledge, let's evaluate the parameters that will determine your chances of success.

Some of the questions you should ask yourself include:

1. Do I have all the necessary training and licenses to perform the duties required to sell my product(s)?

The real estate industry is one that requires continual training, and it's also highly regulated, so you must be certain to keep up with all applicable rules and regulations in your area. You should be in touch with the appropriate commissions and boards in your area to be sure your activities are always in compliance.

2. Have I associated myself with the very best company that handles my type of product?

My advice on this is to shop around. Read the local papers, talk to other agents, ask for references, and so on. Look for a firm with a solid track record and a stellar reputation for performance and integrity.

3. Have I joined all the important organizations that will give me credibility in my community?

I'd recommend that you explore the professional organizations and associations, such as the chamber of commerce in your area, which exist in part to help business people like you with networking. It is also advisable to get involved with charitable work in an area that genuinely interests you. Don't hesitate to volunteer! It's an invaluable way to meet new people, gain credibility, and demonstrate both your skills and your personal characteristics to others in your community.

4. Am I totally prepared to answer most if not all questions that a customer may have regarding my product?

Again, my best advice is to learn everything there is to know about your product through reading, research, interviews, site visits, seminars, conferences, whatever it takes. There is simply no substitute for doing your homework.

5. Can I realistically support my family financially until receiving the projected commissions due me on sales?

Only you and your spouse can answer this one. Suffice to say that you'll need about six months' savings for living expenses to tide you over. Even if you start making sales immediately, real estate does not close quickly in most cases.

6. Am I truly confident of my success?

If you hesitated or answered no to this question, my advice is *don't do it*. Remember, you won't see success until you believe in it. Confidence is the key ingredient for success. You must go into your new business venture with the idea that you are going to be successful, and that it is only a matter of time.

In evaluating your chance of success, you really need to take personal stock of your own abilities and strengths. For example, my own background in stocks, bonds, construction, and sales led me to take a more ambitious approach to real estate listings and sales than another type of person might have attempted. After completing the necessary apprenticeship in the real estate business, I realized where my niche would be, and that was in working to assemble projects. I knew I couldn't complete the deal on my own, but I could excel at doing the initial legwork—identifying and assembling the land, planning the basic project outlines and determining its marketability—before I would need financial help from outside sources.

It's amazing what you can do when you actually set your mind to it. When I started out, I had no cash to speak of; I had arrived only a few years before in Destin, Florida, with $15 in cash, a $5,000 credit card, a car, and my family (consisting of my wife, my 6-year-old son and two dogs). I was given a 300-square-foot guest house where I could live rent free, along with a commissioned job that offered no draw in the real estate business. Because I was new to the real estate business, I also had to apply for my license. Despite what some people would see as obstacles, I was determined to go the distance and bring a real estate project to the point of financing by a serious investor.

It's important to recognize that talking about starting a project to an investor is not the same as taking a fully prepared project to an investor. There's a world of difference between a good idea and a solid, well-researched plan.

Once I had completed the basic homework on a project, such as developing a rough layout, having the land options in hand, having pro formas completed, and obtaining written indications of interest in purchase of the finished product, only then could I solicit the help I needed to carry it through to completion. Thanks to my initial groundwork, I was able to turn my project over to an experienced developer with the resources necessary for getting it done.

All my projects have been accomplished on the theory that if I develop a plan for a product, prove the existence of a market for that product, and show a realistic and profitable projected return, then I should be able to attract the necessary funds and talent to bring the product to fruition.

My very first plan on my own involved the development and sale of more than $200 million worth of condominiums; each new plan that followed was of an even greater scale and value. At the time, my wife, Josette, thought I had lost my mind.

"Where are you going to get the money for that?" she would ask.

My reply was always, "Don't worry about it. The money will come!"

Within only two and one half years, my new plans totaled more than three-quarter billion dollars involving more than 2,000 units. Now, three and one half years later, my planned and ongoing developments exceed $3 billion in value.

What I'm really saying is that if you set your mind to achieve something, you can do it, as long as you have the knowledge and guts to carry it through.

Establishing Your Credibility: Just the Facts

A critical element in establishing your credibility to potential clients is to be honest and show what you are projecting in gains based on past performance of real estate in comparable situations or areas. Back up your claims with hard, reliable data. Being prepared with the right information will help overcome any doubts your clients may have.

Present your clients with charts, graphs, and past performance reports in a format they can easily read and digest, and then take home with them. Be sure and tell them these are only projections based on past performance, and remind them that no one can predict the future.

I can't stress enough the importance of being honest and trustworthy in all your dealings; disclose everything you know and be honest about what you don't know. Don't tell people what you think they want to hear.

Surely the leading motivator for most potential investors is when they say, "Show me the money," and you prove that you can. After all, money is the driving force behind the decisions of all buyers, sellers, and investors. To be successful, you have to show someone what he can potentially expect to make. For example, a local appraiser made a study of the courthouse records and during the 10 previous years it showed waterfront condominiums appreciated on the average as much as 20 percent, 30 percent, and 50 percent in some of those years, but no less than 20 percent each year.

I have included a chart to show how you make up to 296 percent on your money through leveraging your condominium purchase deposits. This chart uses only a 10 percent appreciation factor:

CONDO VALUE

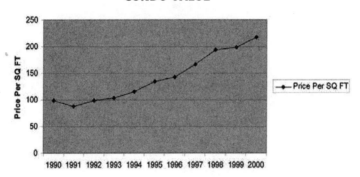

When it comes to selling someone on an investment, no amount of cheerful projection can replace actual numbers, presented in black and white.

CHAPTER 11

IDENTIFYING YOUR MARKET

All real estate products have advantages and disadvantages, so let's talk about them. Whatever type of real estate you decide to sell, your goal should be to become totally knowledgeable about that particular product. If it's waterfront homes, you need to find out what and who the competition is, and then do better. If it's condominiums, you have to do the same as I did. If it's low-cost housing, you need to identify the right locations, scope out your competition, and determine which areas are the lowest priced and why.

Armed with this knowledge, you can not only sell customers what they think they want, but you can also convince them of the value of what you have to offer. So if a customer comes along asking for something you don't have, you're equipped with the knowledge to persuade him or her to consider whatever it is you do have to sell.

In real estate, you should always strive to be on top of market trends. You want to be on the front end of the train, not coming in at the tail end with the caboose! It's sort of like the herd mentality on Wall Street, where the last one gets the worst of the deal. In real estate, when you come in at the tail end of a trend, your customers are going to pay top dollar for the land. And when your customers have to pay top dollar for the land, that means you're going to have to charge top dollar for your units. When you have to list your units for top dollar, and buyers have to pay top dollar for them, that leaves little or no room for your investors to make money.

The key is to focus on one specific market and get to know every aspect of it. When you've attained that level of expertise, you'll build the kind of comfort level with your customers that is invaluable for a salesperson.

If, on the other hand, you try to present yourself as a jack-of-all-trades, selling residential homes, preconstruction condominiums, commercial, and waterfront properties, you are most likely shortchanging your customers. Instead of being extremely proficient and knowledgeable about one specific product, you'll probably only know a little bit about a lot of complicated products. In order to adequately represent a buyer, you must provide the specific information he or she will need to make an educated decision.

You need to become a master of the game!

Rolling out Your Game Plan

Now that you know why you have a blueprint in place, and you have surveyed the full spectrum of the real estate market, why not turn all your energies toward something that will make you the most money?

I have found in my own experience that it's easier to sell a very expensive product than to sell something cheap. This is because the prospective buyers of an expensive product, for example, a pricey parcel of real estate, usually have the money available and are ready to buy, whereas prospective buyers of lower-cost commodities frequently have to struggle with financing issues before they can make a purchase. Not only does this make for a more drawn-out, time-consuming process for you, but it also means a much smaller commission per sale. So you'll end up doing more work for the same or less reward.

While beginning to identify your own real estate market, you'll need to take a poll. Make appointments with different real estate agents specializing in the market you have in mind and bring a list of questions.

Here are a few things you may want to ask:

- Why have you chosen to sell this type real estate?

113

- Why have you chosen this particular geographical area?

- How much time does it take for an average sale?

- What's your closing ratio? Is this higher or lower than average?

- What is the range of commission paid on this type of property?

- Are there resale opportunities?

- How difficult is it to list this type of property?

- Can you give me a commission percentage range at which I can expect to list property?

- Is there heavy competition in your marketing area?

- Who is your competition, and how strong are they?

I would recommend arranging these questions in columns so you can enter the data in an easily readable format, and then make comparisons to determine which properties are the easiest to list, the fastest to sell, and the most profitable for you.

Here is one of my favorite real estate sayings: "If you have a product where the selling is all downhill, why would you want to sell something that's all uphill?"

Bearing this in mind, you may want to consider the viability of multiple-unit sales as an investment vehicle for your customers. If it seems viable in your area, my advice would be to pursue multiple sales, which increases your volume and income dramatically, without much additional work.

After careful consideration of the real estate industry, my own decision to specialize in and target the condominium market was based on analyzing the available data. I chose the preconstruction condominium market because:

- Condominium unit prices were high and climbing, which allowed for large commissions on each sale.

- Multiple sales to one customer were very possible, leading to double and even triple commissions with one customer.

- Resales of units after their construction were often possible.

- Sales could be made over the telephone, a big improvement over the labor intensive face-to-face method of showing property.

- I could make numerous sales by telephone in a single day, rather than taking several days to show and sell just one existing property.

- My personal production volume could expand exponentially, which in turn would create excitement among my associates and customers.

Because excitement can cause a person to exceed his or her abilities, I found myself achieving even more than I had imagined. And it could happen to you, too.

Florida's Emerald Coast

I chose to focus on the Emerald Coast of Florida for my developments because it seemed to have all the ingredients for success:

- A naturally beautiful setting.

- Recent "discovery" of the area by people from all over the world, who were beginning to flock there.

- Increasing demand from the large influx of Baby Boomers who were looking for waterfront (or near waterfront) retirement and vacation homes.

116

- A finite amount of available waterfront land, which was creating a forced and prolonged upsurge in price.

- The waterfront land that was already occupied mostly housed dilapidated, 30- to 40-year-old homes, along with hotels, motels, and restaurants, many of which were prime for demolition.

The Emerald Coast encompasses approximately 120 miles of Gulf-front property with some of the whitest sands in the world; it looks almost exactly like white ground sugar. In fact, it's so white that even at midday in 100°F weather, it is cool to the feet. The water is a gorgeous, emerald shade of green nearly all the time, and the offshore and inshore fishing is abundant. Unlike most coastal regions in the United States, this area had very few high-rise structures with only moderate development in the past.

With all of these factors in its favor, it didn't take long for developers, real estate agents, and buyers to take notice of the Emerald Coast. Aggressive development began in Destin, Florida, in the late 1980s and early 1990s, around the same time the area of Gulf Shores, Alabama, was starting to rebuild the areas decimated years earlier by Hurricane Camille. Although I don't believe in the notion of luck, at least, not without hard work to create it, I can say looking back that the timing of my move to this area was ideal.

It's been reported that every seven seconds one of 76 million Baby Boomers turn 55, and that this trend will continue through at least 2012. If this is true, and many of these Boomers are indeed looking for waterfront properties to retire to, then I'm sitting on a solid gold mine, as long as I can continue to supply new waterfront, near waterfront, or amenity-laden resort condominiums.

Of course, all gold mines eventually run out of gold, at which point the mining company must seek out other options. In the early 1990s, both Destin and Gulf Shores had miles of potential waterfront land ripe for the picking. Now there is far less of it left, and most of what's left has been priced to the max or restricted in some way. That's why I am presently seeking other locations for future condominium sales.

Gulf Shores, Alabama, had become a real estate hot spot in recent years, until all the land there was bought and developed, and there was simply no more available. Developers had to move further east to Destin and Perdido Key, Florida; and after those areas were built out, Okaloosa Island became the next hot spot. Now that Okaloosa Island is built out, where will developers go next? Panama City Beach, Florida. And where will they go from there? No one can say for sure, because most of the waterfront property in the United States has already been bought, sold, and developed.

With less and less waterfront land available in the United States, it appears that future developers will need to look overseas for new opportunities. That's why I hope to begin my first international project somewhere in the Caribbean or in Mexico. After studying the phenomenal movement of the condominium markets in the United States, I began to suspect that the Cabo, Mexico, region will soon be comparable to the well-known tourist area of Cancun. It is my educated projection that at some point not far in the future this area is going to explode.

Now you have an even better idea of why I chose to specialize in the preconstruction condominium market. It's my preference because of the multifold potential for my customers, for my investors, and of course for me, too. In your career, you need to decide what area of real estate works best for you.

You, the Power Broker

Becoming a true "power broker" takes time, attention, and knowledge. Buying and selling preconstruction condos that are controlled by others for your customers and yourself can help you become a millionaire and power broker. But if you want to become what I call a super power broker, you need to go a few steps further. Here are my 10 simple rules for achieving that goal:

1. Get your real estate license. You may want to obtain licenses in other resort areas as well; there are plenty of additional real estate opportunities outside the perimeter of your local subdivisions.

119

2. Become familiar with and active in your own real estate market as well as other resort-type markets nationally and internationally.

3. Study the market value of the product you want to sell. You'll get further insights into what lies ahead for your local market by studying the markets of similar cities and resorts.

4. Find experienced people who can help you learn about assembling land for different types of development. When you assemble land for a project and go forward with ideas for developing that project, you can control the deal with very little investment on your part. With the proper written protections of nondisclosure and noncompete agreements, you can move forward with a project without fear of someone taking it from you.

You'll find that you can demand much higher commissions and possibly even secure part ownership in the project by controlling the deal. At this point you may also demand that you control the listings of the end products of your project. That's when you start to become a super power broker!

5. Select a property and/or parcels of land. Almost any parcel of land is suited for something beneficial or attractive to an investor. Use your head and consider what would be the most attractive and profitable uses for that land. Select parcels that you know would fit into your arena of knowledge, such as condos, apartments, or single-family homes. Obviously, if you know nothing about commercial projects, don't select a commercially zoned parcel. Stick to what you know or what you want to know.

6. Determine the highest and most efficient use for your property. For example, if you had a 600-foot shoreline on a parcel of oceanfront property, would it be better to put one large house on it or 300 condos?

7. Determine the best layout for the project on the land. Among the various considerations are property ingress and egress, views, and so on. A good architect can be helpful with this.

8. List all the amenities you want to include in a project, such as pools, restaurants, boutique shops, spas, and so forth.

9. Take your ideas to a reputable architect. If possible, find one that "bets on the come," meaning he or she will get paid if the project comes together. Ask the architect to create a rough rendering of your ideas; together you will decide how many units, what size they should be, and if there is any commercial use applicable.

10. Prepare what is known as a pro forma. This document shows your projected cost and profit figures for the project and will allow you and your potential investors to determine the overall viability of the project.

You should know that not all pro formas are identical. You may find there are some items on my sample that you don't need, or other things missing that you need to add, so be sure to look them over carefully. If you don't have experience in a particular area, such as cost, locate some-one who's an expert in that field. (Hint: Your architect may be able to help you figure in some of the costs.) You can also talk to other area developers to find out what they have calculated as the cost per square foot on the building itself.

Most of the time when I talk about figuring the cost per square foot of a condo development, I mean everything it takes to build that condominium inside the footprint of that building (nothing on the outside of it). All the outside fea-tures, like landscaping, pool, tennis courts, and so on, are con-sidered extras, and should be listed on your pro forma. Once you have gathered and researched all these figures, you have a good idea of what it's going to cost.

This is the time to figure out what to charge as your sale price for each unit. So you'll need to have a separate part of your pro forma that's listed as an "income" section. The income section will identify not only the type of units that you're putting in the building, but also what they will sell for per square foot.

Once you've added it all up, you'll be able to project your net profits by deducting your costs from your expected sales proceeds. On the pro forma, you must also figure all of the interest that will have to be paid on the money you put into the project as of the date you put it in. Figure 1 shows my standard pro forma, where you'll find a place for each entry required.

Opportunity Is a Fleeting Chance for Success

Opportunities of one kind or another present themselves to us in some form on an almost daily basis, but most opportunities are overlooked for a variety of reasons:

- Lack of recognition.

- Lack of interest.

- Lack of confidence.

- Lack of time.

Truly great opportunities are fleeting by nature, so you must be prepared to make swift and determined decisions in order to take advantage of them. I have trained myself to do two things swiftly: recognize opportunities and react immediately with an informed decision. If you don't react quickly, your great opportunity will pass you by.

One example of this is my Panama City Beach Developments, which I began to work on just as soon as I realized that the land in Destin, Okaloosa Island, and Gulf Shores was quickly disappearing.

In the summer of 2001, I was asked to visit **Panama City Beach**, Florida, approximately 40 miles from my home in Destin, to determine the marketability and viability of building a 33-story condominium project on the beach there. For years Panama City Beach has been a destination resort for millions of people in the Southeast. Over time, the region's

COST	Phase I	Dev. Fee Items
Condominium Project		
Date		
Land Cost	$ -	
Land payments not applied to purchase	$ -	
Land subordinated to construction loan	$ -	
Seed Money Input	$ -	
Construction Condos (H/A sf @ $xxx.00 sf) includes owners lounge, exercise	$ -	$ -
Construction pool for Phase 1 (5,000 s.f. @ $xxx)	$ -	$ -
Construction Commercial	$ -	$ -
Architectural, incl. Elec. Mech. and Structural Eng. @ .xxx%	$ -	
Sewer&Water(1BR@$xxxx 2BR@$xxxx 3BR@$xxxx)	$ -	$ -
Less existing W&S taps	$ -	$ -
Pkg on Grade xxx@$xxxx + xxx structural @$xxxx	$ -	$ -
Checkin and Real Estate Office Furnishings	$ -	$ -
Miscellaneous Start-up (Temp. Signage, setup sales/dev. Office, sewer, water, elect.)	$ -	$ -
Site Work & Infastructure (includes water & sewer extentions and regrading)	$ -	$ -
Demolition & Abatment (includes asbestos disposal)	$ -	$ -
Phase 1 inspection of property	$ -	$ -
Signage for completed project	$ -	$ -
2 each Spas (xxx sf. @ $xxx x 2each)	$ -	$ -
Pool xxxx s.f. @ $xxx	$ -	$ -
Pool Furniture (incl. Lounges, tables, chairs, bar stools, umbrellas and gen. area seating)	$ -	
Pool Fence and Project Fence (x' aluminum) xxx lineal feet @ $xx + x gates @ $xx	$ -	$ -
Survey & Topo (includes final survey	$ -	$ -
Landscaping (incl. palms, segos, ground cover, water gardens, sprinkler syst	$ -	$ -
Renderings/Models	$ -	
Permitting	$ -	$ -
Soils Testing	$ -	$ -
Geo Testing and Auger Piles	$ -	$ -
Civil Engineering	$ -	$ -
Structural Engineering	$ -	
Professional fees for DEP Apps	$ -	
DEP Applications (xxx units phase 1 @ $xxx)	$ -	$ -
Preliminary Costs (incl. Land contracts, Investor Contracts, CD production and Misc.)	$ -	
Land and Loan Closing Cost	$ -	
On-Site Sales/Development Office and Furnishings (Temporary)	$ -	
Interim Operations (xx months @ $xx,xxx) Incl. Gen.Office Exp., Acctg, Utilities,	$ -	
Salaries for Office Help and active operatives	$ -	
Legal/Condominium Documents (Incl. Documents submission and approval, HOA	$ -	
Budget, Dep permit labor for Set-Back Line	$ -	
Builders Risk Insurance (Buy Down)	$ -	$ -
Health Center & Gym xxxx s.f. (equipment and furnishings)	$ -	
Owners Lounge & Kitchen xxxx s.f. (incl furnishings	$ -	
Entrance & Roads etc. (possible turn lanes improved and electronic parking gates)	$ -	$ -
Inspections (includes all required building inspections by city, etc.)	$ -	$ -
Telephone Lines & Transformers (Allowance for relocating or reinstalling	$ -	$ -
Advertising	$ -	
Brochures (Incl. the design and printing of several thousand Project Brochures)	$ -	
Miscellaneous	$ -	$ -
Water Intrusion Expert Inspections	$ -	$ -
Misc. Project Equipment (Incl. lawnmowers, tractors for garbage pulling, golf carts,	$ -	
maids carts, speakers and amp systems, survelance systems, seating for	$ -	
public areas, Tools for maintenance, cabinets for concierge and valet stations		
and electronic equipment as needed for checkin and out, etc.		
Developer fee	0	
Construction Manager	0	
Investor Finder Fees	$ -	
Sales Bonuses (Allowance)	$ -	
COST SUB TOTAL	$ -	$ -
Interest (80% of the Phase Cost x .060 x .60 x 2.00)	$ -	
Interest on Interest (Interest Cost x .060 x 2.00)	$ -	
Points to Lender @ 1%	$ -	
Interest on Points (Point Cost x .060 x 2.00)	$ -	
Total Cost	$ -	

Fig. 1

124

Condominium Project

xx stories of condos & Structural Parking	Type	Number Each P1	P2	SF	TSF P1	TSF P2	$ Per SF	Unit Cost	Phase III
(Examples)					Total S.F.				
3BR 3B Penthouse Corner	A.-Penthouse Corner	x	0	xxxx	xxxx	xxxx	xxx	xxxxx	xxxxxxx
3BR 3B Corner	B-Penthouse Ctr	x		xxxx	xxxx	xxxx	xxx	xxxxxx	xxxxxxx
3BR 3B	C - Corner	x	0	xxxx	xxxx	xxxx	xxx	xxxxxx	xxxxxxx
3BR 3B	D- Interior	x	0	xxxx	xxxx	xxxx	xxx	xxxxxx	xxxxxxx
	Total number of units	xxx			Total footage				
Commercial and Common area of building incl. Owners Lounge & Exercise Room					xxx				
Total Air Conditioned Area					xxx			Total Sales	xxxxxxxxxx

PROJECTIONS ON SELLING THE BUILDING:

Phase I

Show selling the following number of units then increase price		xxxx							xxxxxxx
Increase of x% after for the next number of units		xxxx							xxxxxxx
Parking Spaces	xxx	sell xxx each					at	xxxxx	xxxxxx
Total Sales for Phase I							Gross Sales		xxxxxxxxxx

Gross Sales	xxxxxxxxxx
Less x% R.E. commission	xxxxxxxx
Total	xxxxxxxx
Less Title Ins	xxxx
Total	xxxxxxxxxx
Less Cost to Build	xxxxx
Less Repay Seed Money+x%	xxxxx
Net Profit	**xxxxx**
Percentage	**xxx%**
on cost	

hotels, motels, and restaurants have aged and fallen into disrepair, making the area prime for new development.

In my brief visit, I had begun to explore an experimental preconstruction sales effort. In a five-week period, I sold approximately $6 million worth of preconstruction condos for the developer, proving the viability and marketability of the proposed project.

The remaining waterfront land wasn't vacant, but was populated with 30- to 40-year-old homes, as well as hotels, motels, and restaurants, that were prime for demolition.

Excited and armed with all this information, I explored the area and located a 450-foot stretch of beach containing a 40-year-old motel, for which I made an offer to purchase on option. Once I had the first piece under option, I pursued the surrounding properties on a similar option agreement.

Over the previous few years I had helped plenty of other wannabe developers put deals together, but had never ventured out on my own like this. The wording of the option to purchase agreement put me at little, if any, risk, while still giving me the opportunity to control the deal, list the property, and participate in ownership of the project. At that time I only had $30,000 that I could comfortably put up as an earnest money deposit for the entire project.

The Panama City project is now becoming a reality. My wife never dreamed that I could actually pull this off with only a total of $25,000 personal (not at risk) investment. What began as a $160 million project became a $200 million project.

Once I had all the land option contracts in hand and firm, I began the marketing program to sell the first-phase units on reservation agreement. An architect friend agreed to "bet on the come" for his fees and make the required preliminary drawings to help with sales. In short order, we had half of the first phase sold, proving a viable and marketable project. Now I had something substantial to sell to an investor with the desire and the money to come into the project and see it completed.

Note that there are several things you must do before you sell interest in the development company you have initiated yourself:

1. If the property you purchased for the company was listed, make sure you are on the contract as the selling agent, in order for the bank to pay you a commission at the issue of the construction loan.

2. If the property isn't listed, then be sure to list the property before you buy it.

3. If the owner doesn't want to pay a commission, then add a commission to the amount that he or she wants so you can make a one-time, one-person listing. This will give you recognized sales volume that can be touted to your peers and to potential customers. It will also allow you to receive income at the closing of the construction loan, even if you end up selling the project to others.

4. Sell a percentage of interest to a well-funded and experienced developer. The sale price should account for the developer putting up all of the money required to bring the project to fruition and signing on the construction loan. This will relieve you of most of the developer duties and allow you to move on to other projects.

5. Before selling the project to someone else, write a real estate listing agreement with the entity you set up to control the development to cover all of the units in the project until final completion. This will also give you future listing and sale benefits.

Once I had this project in hand, I immediately started looking for the next opportunity, which I found only a quarter mile down the beach. I quickly acquired the central piece of property, then set about gathering the other, smaller pieces surrounding it. This $220 million project broke ground in May 2004; my total investment (not at risk) was $30,000.

Okay, you probably can see where I'm going with this: Suddenly, I had evolved from a successful real estate agent to a successful developer or codeveloper. In both positions, maintaining momentum is key to success. Landowners only recognize those developers who actually do what they set out to do. They'll be far more willing to grant the terms you request on a contract when they know you are successful.

To keep my momentum going, I searched the area further and picked up enough properties for a third, $250 million development, before the onslaught of new developers could arrive and invade the market.

This development broke ground in December of 2004. My total up-front (not at risk) investment was $16,100. The value of my total projects under contract now amounted to $670 million, and I had only $71,000 (mostly refundable money) invested in the land. I guess now you will say that if all I started with was $30,000, where did I get the rest of it? Answer: I made sales commissions on regular real estate properties during this whole process. You will have to do the same.

Success Breeds Success!

There is no telling where this progression will end. I now have people bringing me projects to list, sell, or develop all the time. One I'll discuss here is Caribbean Lake, a proposed projected $200 million project that "fell into my lap" because someone out there felt I had the knowledge to get it sold and built. I say it fell into my lap because instead of seeking out this project on my own, this time I was invited to determine what the project should be and to put the entire deal together. Someone who had seen my previous success decided that I must know what I am doing, and therefore that I was a solid bet. Do not expect all proposed projects to come to fruition!

When you've acquired the necessary personal knowledge, experience, and confidence to do this, you will be on your way to being a multimillionaire.

Maximum Profit With Minimum Risks

What entity gives the best tax benefits? How can I limit my liability? These are common questions posed by both beginning and experienced real estate investors. Following are some answers to common questions about maximizing profit and limiting liability in real estate investing.

How Should I Take Title?

The first and biggest mistake you can make as an investor is taking title in your own name. Because all deeds are public record and free for prying eyes to see, having property in your own name makes you an easy target for tenants, creditors, and attorneys. If a liability is created on your property, you, the owner, are liable. So make sure you have a buffer zone between you and your properties by keeping your ownership private.

The simplest, most effective device for taking title is called a land trust, also known as the Illinois Land Trust. The land trust is a form of revocable, living trust used to take title to real estate. This way the trust, rather than you, can assume liability for loans. Using a different trust for each property (e.g., The 2537 Clarkson Street Trust) allows you to own, manage, and transfer property with anonymity.

Keeping a low profile is very important for investors who don't want the whole world to know their business. Land trust agreements aren't recorded in any public register, so the beneficiaries of the trust are not easily discoverable. The beneficiaries of a land trust can be you, a corporation, or some other entity. The trust itself is not considered a separate taxable entity from the beneficiaries (see Internal Revenue Code (I.R.C.) Sec 671-678). Thus, there are no tax consequences for transferring a property into or out of a land trust.

Advantages to Corporations

A land trust is an effective device for taking title, but it will not protect the beneficiaries from personal liability. Because the beneficiary of a land trust reserves the right to direct the actions of the trustee, the beneficiaries can be held liable for mishaps on the property. Thus, if you are seeking to "buy and flip" property, you'll want the beneficiary of the trust to be a corporation in order to limit your liability.

Establishing a corporation will also limit the problem of IRS dealer status. A dealer is someone who regularly buys and sells real estate as a business. Once an individual is tagged as a dealer, the profits on his or her sale of property are subject to self-employment tax (approximately 15 percent). Corporate dividends, on the other hand, are not subject to self-employment tax, although the investor may have to take some salary, subject to self-employment tax, to satisfy the IRS requirements.

C and S Corporations

For tax purposes, there are essentially two types of corporations. A corporation is a C corporation by default; whereas S status must be elected. A C corporation files its own tax return and pays taxes on its profits. When the corporation distributes profit to its shareholders, called a dividend, the shareholders pay additional tax on their personal income tax returns, called double taxation. An S corporation is not taxed at the corporate level. Like a partnership, it files an informational return and the shareholders report their shares of profit or loss on their personal income tax returns.

Which Corporation Is Better for Real Estate?

The answer depends on an investor's particular tax situation. For example, an investor with a working spouse may benefit from an S corporation, because a loss from the corporation's operations can be used to offset the working spouse's income. On the other hand, if an investor has a large profit, he or she will owe income tax on all profits, whether or not they are reinvested or distributed. With a C corporation, the individual shareholder is not taxed on profits until they are distributed; the corporation itself pays tax on its income, but the first $50,000 of C corporation income is only taxed at the rate of 15 percent, which is much lower than personal income tax rates.

In most cases, it makes sense to start out with an S corporation, then create a second C corporation when the tax advantages of a C corporation are preferable for you.

Limited Liability Corporations (LLCs)

The limited liability company, or LLC, is now recognized in all 50 states. People often confuse an LLC with a corporation, but it functions much more like a partnership. Its owners, called members, can participate equally in the management of the company without personal liability.

An LLC, if it has two or more members, is treated as a partnership for federal income tax purposes. Thus, similar to an S corporation, the profits and losses flow through to its owners. On rental activities, these profits are not subject to self-employment tax. An LLC that engages in buying and flipping may subject the members to self-employment tax, so a corporation may be better than an LLC for this purpose.

Most states now recognize single-member LLCs, which are LLCs with only one owner. The IRS treats a single member LLC as a nonentity for tax purposes. That means the member would report as though the LLC did not exist. Thus, if the investor was reporting his rental activities on Schedule E of his federal income tax return, a transfer of property from his own name to a single member LLC would not result in any change of reporting. Furthermore, an LLC between husband and wife can still be treated as a single member for federal income tax purposes. Thus, one could form an LLC for each property he owns and still file only one tax return!

"Sandwich" Lease/Options

When you lease with option, then sublease with option, also known as a "sandwich," you are essentially doing a buy and flip. That is, when your subtenant exercises, you simultaneously exercise from the owner, then sell to the subtenant. A corporation may be better than an LLC in this situation, especially if you do a high volume of deals and risk being classified as a dealer.

Land Trust Corporation Versus LLC

The land trust is simply a title-holding device, not an entity apart from its owner. Thus, regardless of who the beneficiary is, the property should always be bought and sold in a land trust. The beneficiary should be a corporation for short-term deals and an LLC for long-term rentals.

When Do I Create a Land Trust?

Logistically, I prefer to use my corporation to sign the contract as a buyer. If the contract for any reason goes bad, I'd rather the seller sue my corporation than sue me directly. When it comes time to close, I simply create the land trust, then assign the contract from my corporation to the trust.

Should I Use One Land Trust for Each Property?

Yes, it's best to have a different trust for each property to enhance privacy and prevent someone from figuring out a pattern of activity.

Options Versus Reservations

An option is a legally binding contract; a reservation isn't binding, because neither party can enforce it. Reservations are designed so that either party in a proposed property transaction has the flexibility to back out without a great hassle. All the buyer has to do is request his or her deposit back. The same applies to the developer; if he or she has made a mistake on the estimate, there's an option to back out and start over again.

Options are almost never offered on a condominium prior to going to hard contract, which means you have all contracts signed and deposits in. This is what the lending bank will require for you to get a construction loan issued and begin that work. Hard contract is a binding, or purchase, contract. It is officially a subscription purchase agreement allowing you to build a condominium for a designated purchaser.

If a builder has to back out of the reservation, the buyer will get his or her deposit back plus interest, if applicable. Ethically, the developer can't just back out for no reason; there must be a legitimate reason, such as a change in the size of a stack of units. In this case, the cost would have to go up so the developer would have to cancel the agreements and ask the purchaser if he or she would like to sign up again at the new size and price.

CHAPTER 12

LOCATING SUITABLE PROPERTY

Now that we've come this far, it's time to take another look at the old cliché of "location, location, location." Where do you find properties capable of turning a profit for everyone involved? I've always been told that if you're going to sell something, you should sell something expensive because your commissions are bigger and you have fewer sales to make overall. This means less work and more profits earned for you.

Take the restaurant business, for example. A four-star restaurant with high prices only has to serve 10 customers to make a certain profit, with relatively little work required from the server. A fast-food chain, on the other hand, has to sell its products to 100 customers to earn the same amount of profit, and the fast-food servers have to do 10 times the amount of work! See my point?

I didn't want to distract from the deal earlier, but in fact the old saying about location is absolutely true. In a desirable location, your property appreciation tends to be greater, even though you pay more for your property up front; and your sales are quicker so you incur less interest on your construction loan. So why not go downhill instead of uphill? If you always buy in the best locations, you shouldn't have a problem in reselling even if the prices are high. Whether you work in residential or commercial real estate, people will always be on the lookout for a great location.

When visiting San Diego, California, recently, I observed what I thought was an unusual phenomenon in condominium sales. Developers were actually locating condo units in the downtown area, renovating old, dilapidated buildings where safety had once been a major concern. Now, however, the renovation of the downtown area had caused property values to soar. Thanks to the improved street lighting, security measures, new sidewalks, and new businesses opening, sales and prices had gone through the roof.

In my area, the prime location for condominiums is on the Gulf Shore. Around here, everyone who keeps up with the condo market knows that I have some of the very best locations. Although the properties here are expensive, there are many advantages to these prime, desirable locations. Demand for this product will be much higher, which means higher sales prices, shortened marketing periods, less advertising, and possibly higher profits for the investors. So it does pay to look at location in your investments.

Still, location shouldn't be your sole consideration in purchasing property for a project. You should be sure to consider the zoning regulations, and find an area that's conducive for your proposed type of construction (mid-rises, highrises, townhouses, and so on). You need to know what the regulations are in that county before you secure the land, otherwise you might be wasting your time.

For example, Bay County, Florida, has enacted regulations that make it difficult to get permits to construct highrise condominiums, and most of the residents in that county are strongly opposed to seeing them built. So why go uphill when you can go downhill? By contrast, Panama City Beach has welcomed developers to help rebuild the Gulf-front portions of its city.

Once you have selected your property, you must determine whether your project is financially viable by estimating the cost and profitability of the project. As I mentioned, this work-up is called a "pro forma" (see Figure 1 on page 124). Fill in this form using your personal knowledge and that of associated professionals and potential subcontractors.

When you have the completed pro forma in hand, you'll be ready to secure the necessary seed money for initially funding the project. You will also have established a time line for the project, according to the terms you laid out in the purchase contract. This contract will dictate which things you have to have completed by which time. Your purchase contract should allow you sufficient time to determine the viability of a project before having to pay nonrefundable amounts of money.

CHAPTER 13

MARKETING AND SALES TECHNIQUES

Your approach to marketing and sales will vary according to the type of real estate you're involved in buying and selling. In this book, I'm discussing condominium projects with livable residences on the Florida Gulf Coast; but even if you're in another location, chances are many of the same techniques will apply.

First you need to identify all of the pluses of the property and its location. You should also consider every one of the project's amenities, because these are a crucial consideration for most buyers. Try to offer as many amenities as you can to attract the initial investors and find purchasers of the individual units once they are for sale.

If you have an existing database of clients, I recommend giving these customers the first chance at purchasing your new units. Be sure to mail them each a brochure describing the new location, even if it's just a black-and-white picture of what you're trying to do. I've sometimes sold a project sketched on scratch paper, simply because my investors wanted to be first in a project.

Second, I would do a more generalized mailing. If your project represents an investment-type property, which most condominiums can be if marketed that way, I would target my marketing efforts to people who have already purchased investment condominiums. I would prepare an easy-to-read market study of the area with comparisons to similar properties and their values over time, and then do a mailing directly to those people.

Last, I would place large ads in the newspapers and in real estate books. Most real estate agents don't realize the investment potential of residential condominiums such as those on the Gulf Coast. If you look at the way they have appreciated, and the amount of income that can be earned through short-term rentals, there's not much that will match it in today's business world in terms of the return on the amount of cash you have invested. In determining what your market is, you must determine what the value of your property is. If you're selling condominiums, you should determine their price range and what sort of income a person would need in order to buy one.

It's the same as with other kinds of products. If you're going to sell an airplane, for example, you must find someone who can afford it. So where do you find that kind of person? You need to determine who you have around you in your circle of friends and colleagues that can help you with the skills and resources you don't have on your own.

One of the biggest secrets to putting together a deal is to get it in the position where you have power, rather than just being somebody looking for money. In other words, you make your initial investment in it. You put up the initial money and get everything started; even if you don't know how to complete the whole project, you try and get most of it done. Once you've taken the first few steps toward bringing it to fruition, you have something solid to market. That's when you seek your investor and whomever else you might need to bring into the deal to make it successful or to complete it.

When drawing up a contract, bear in mind that these agreements can take on a personality of their own; you just have to give each one the particular slant you want it to have for the particular person with whom you're dealing. A contract is more than merely a black-and-white document. It can also be a sales tool if you design it that way. Much consideration must be paid to your customer when you're writing a contract.

Most people, when beginning to draw up a contract, are only thinking about what they need, when they should really be putting the needs of their customers first. When your customers and partners start reading a contract and can recognize that you have understood and anticipated their concerns in preparing it, their defenses will come down naturally and you'll have a much easier time with your transaction. And remember, when you're asking for investments, good credit and a reputation for integrity are invaluable.

Most real estate agents rely on the same tired, humdrum methods of marketing their products, so your aim should be to come up with a creative and polished approach in order to distinguish both yourself and your project. Like I've said, real estate is in large part show business. If you really show up, you'll get the business.

CHAPTER 14

ATTRACTING INVESTORS

Method I

There is an old saying that you can learn a lot about money by going down to the bank and trying to borrow some. Actually, that's something you'll undoubtedly be doing as a real estate investor: borrowing money. For example, a real estate investor can make an unsecured loan to the company for a return on his investment. This type of loan is usually very hard to get because it's speculative, and you probably don't have a proven track record yet. The best approach is to first offer to bring the investor in as a partner, with you giving him or her a second mortgage on the land behind the institutional lender. Once you've sold your investor on the project, you can then switch the setup of the deal from ownership in the development LLC to a percentage of the profit.

This change allows you to retain total control of the development, and at the same time puts your investor in an arms-length position concerning the development. Just be forewarned, paying someone a percentage of the profit means you have to keep close tabs on what the actual profit of the development is to avoid lawsuits. This means close bookkeeping and a final audit.

To further strengthen your position, once the investor is happy with the projected amount of profit that he or she may make, you can offer to pay that projected profit as a flat fee instead of a percentage of the profit. I go one step further to put the investor totally at ease by also offering to allow him or her to be paid first before any profits are paid to me.

Method II

Method II has a different twist than Method I. Have the investor purchase the land that is to be used in the project. Offer to have him or her purchase the land using the option to purchase contract (see pg. 163) and simultaneously give the investor a contract for you to buy the land from him at a much higher value. This works particularly well in a market where the land values are rapidly escalating because the investor has the land as security for his investment. The setup for this method is as follows:

1. Negotiate the land purchase, putting the contract in your name and/or assigns.

2. Assign the contract to the investor for the original amount of purchase.

3. Have the investor sign a contract or other agreement selling the land back to you or your development company at a much higher price, an amount that the investor will accept.

4. Most investors will not pay cash for the land purchase and will borrow 75 percent, putting down 25 percent.

5. Offer to repay his bank loan plus the 25 percent deposit at the project construction loan issue, leaving the balance of the amount owed to the investor to be subordinated to the construction loan and paid at the completion of the project. This subordination gives you equity in the land that you can show on the proforma.

In order to procure an investor there are a few things you need to do during the due diligence period to prepare the project:

- Determine the floor plans to be used.

- Procure a preliminary site plan.

147

- Determine the number of units that would probably fit on the site plan.

- Produce a pro forma showing the prices of the units, projected cost, and projected profit.

- Produce a schematic, a side view of the building showing the unit number, type of unit, and price of unit.

- Secure a reservation agreement. Reservations are nonbinding letters of intent.

- Start selling the units.

- Once you have a good number of pre-sales and before the due diligence period expires, seek the investor. Now you have something to sell!

Method III

Have the landowner participate in the project by leaving his land in the deal. A scenario could be as follows: Let's say the landowner paid $3 million for the land but he's asking $5 million. Without enticement he probably would not give you very good terms. Most want to close immediately with a very short due diligence period. The way you get what you want in making the deal is to first inform the purchaser that most of the deals that fail, fail for lack of putting in enough time on the contract, and because the project is not good. Before going into negotiations on the land, you must determine the most that you can pay for it. You do this by creating a preliminary pro forma.

Ask yourself this question: Would you really care what you had to pay for the land as long as you can make the amount of profit that you require? If your answer is no, then make this your motto: "It really doesn't matter to me what I have to pay you as a landowner as long as the numbers work." I actually start my negotiation this way. This puts the seller at ease and instills some immediate trust in what you are saying.

Because the value is there according to proforma, you tell your investors that you don't care how much money they make as long as it's reasonable and you can afford it. Once you negotiate the amount of profit to be paid to the landowner, offer to pay an acceptable amount at construction loan closing with the balance subordinated to the construction loan. You can usually get this done if you are actually and ultimately paying more than the property is presently worth in order to get your terms.

Securing a Construction Loan

Financing is a matter of finding who can actually handle the loan amount you need and making that investor feel comfortable about being able to issue the loan. So you may have to shop several places to get your loan. You have to be aware, however, that there are also a lot of sharks out there who want to take your money by asking for big due diligence fees up front for research. Do not pay anyone a fee until you have done your own due diligence on that particular lending firm and you feel comfortable about paying the up-front fees required to secure the loan.

CHAPTER 15

SECURING SEED MONEY

The first step in securing funding for your real estate project is to secure the seed money required to carry the project through to construction loan issue. The seed money is considered equity in the project but is not construction money; it is used for all of the soft costs and any land carrying cost necessary prior to construction loan issue. At the issue of the construction loan, the land is paid either in full or with carryback by the seller(s), and the bank then issues a commencement letter to the builder, who then starts construction on the project.

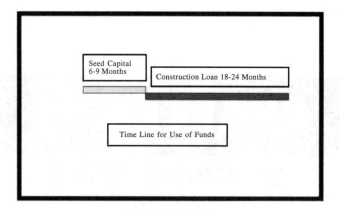

Seed Capital
  1.Option Payments
  2.Engineering
  3.Site Planning
  4.Initial Marketing

Construction Loan
  1.Land Take Down
  2.Project Construction
  3.Project Marketing
  4.Developer Fees

The investors will want to know how their funds will be used; therefore, I place a copy of this list in the investor package and give a copy to the escrow agency that will hold those funds for specific disbursement by invoice.

You may select a seed money investor for many reasons. Your investor may be a passive investor or may be very knowledgeable and have political pull for getting the project permitted. He or she may sign on the construction loan with you or may be a very good developer with experience. I choose to have either a passive investor or a qualified developer/investor. A developer/investor simplifies the whole process but costs you more of the project profits.

When making a deal with a developer/investor, you will need to have a good part of the preliminary work done and have some reservation sales, so that he will not demand too much of the project interest. In other words, have something very enticing and tangible to sell him or he will not think you are deserving of much of the project interest. When big money is involved, you must have everything in writing, even if your partner is a good friend.

In putting the project's land pieces together, you must be aware of what's around you at all times. For example, recently I went into a motel to see if I could buy the property because someone told me it was for sale. But when I walked out, I realized that the property would be a lot better if I could add the property adjacent to it. So rather than go home and just think about that one property, I went next door and talked to those folks. Now if I can put that together, instead of having a 330-unit project, I'll have about a 475-unit project, which makes it a lot more profitable and a lot more worthwhile.

If you have the opportunity, you should always deal with sophisticated, qualified investors. That way, you don't have to spend a great deal of time on the road showing them sites. Always pause when you're making a sales purchase, it tends to make the person you are selling and listening to uncomfortable. So it's really the first person who speaks who is the loser. If you ask a buying question and you wait until you get your answer without saying anything, then you will succeed. When you're building up investors to sell them something as an investment, you ask them to buy something for twice what you think they can afford. What you're really doing is stretching their minds. They're thinking, "I can't do that! But I might be able to do this, which is half as much." They're thinking one unit, and I tell them four, so they elect to stay in the middle at two.

Many times when somebody is making a sale, the buyers are already sold. But that particular salesperson will just keep on and on. As a result, the buyers get bored listening, and it makes them feel not interested anymore. Now the sale is destroyed. So whenever you know somebody's sold, stop and take the money. Selling can be learned. You can go to college and learn how to sell. But in reality, selling is in your heart and in what you feel you can accomplish.

In other words, if you believe in what you're selling, it's easy. But if you're selling something that you don't believe in, then it's really hard. So don't ever sell anything you don't believe in. That way you won't have to go uphill. Millionaires are largely made in their own minds, not necessarily by following this step or that step.

You are a millionaire when you believe you are. Whatever you believe you are, you can be. But you have to have some kind of venue or some kind of vehicle to get you there. So pick something you really enjoy make your millions. The easiest and most enjoyable route for me is real estate.

Real estate is one of the greatest things for wealth that's ever been in United States because of the amount of land available. So why not pick the easy track and go with real estate? The way you get people's attention is not necessarily with your length of tenure, but with what you're doing. If you put the right deal together or are able to show people how much money they can actually make, then you have a deal. You don't have to be an expert as long as you check your figures, know that your pro forma is correct, and know that you're giving investors and buyers the correct information.

Even as a novice in real estate, you can go out and get professional help to put together your project and still make big money. You just have to get the right people together to help you. Even if you don't have the money to accomplish a project entirely on your own, try to go as far as you can without help. That's what I do. In other words, go far enough to show lenders and investors the progress you've made. Do this, and the money is easier to come by.

Goal setting is a learned thing, and the way you learn is to practice it. After all, nobody ever accomplishes anything of consequence without a goal. I think goal setting is the strongest human force available for self-motivation. How do you start? I get up in the morning and I think, "What's the most important thing I have to do today?" It's very important that you achieve everything you decide you're going to achieve in that day. If you don't do it, then do it the next day, because these are important steps to success.

155

Everybody should set his own goals, whether he does it in his mind or in his book. You should also have a book, a daily planner, where you actually put down all the thoughts you have for that day so that later you can go back and see what you did. I found that something I did four months earlier might become a very crucial event. If I didn't have a record of it, how could I remember it?

Everything you do ultimately comes in a circle. If you treat somebody badly, if you're not fair, or if you lie, it will always come back to you. If you did good, it will come back to you in a good way. If you lied, it will come back to you and hurt you. It always happens that way.

Most real estate folks look at deals where $100,000 here or there make all the difference in the world. But in reality, the bigger the deal, the easier it is to put together. And the reason it's easier is because you're dealing with qualified people who can afford the investments, and there's a lot more profit involved. Therefore, the financial institutions look at it differently and so do the investors. The bigger your deal, the more people want to be involved because the profit is bigger. Also, when you're putting big deals together there's more risk, but you're dealing with people who have the funds and can afford that risk. So if you deal with those people and the project is successful, the profits from that are substantially higher than dealing on low-budget projects.

I used to think that $1 million was a lot of money. Many people think $1 million is a lot of money, and it is. But when you start dealing in million-dollar projects, $1 million becomes like a dollar bill. I'm presently dealing in a $3.1 billion project that would scare the pants off even Bill Gates at the outset. But it doesn't scare me because I know that the profit is there. I know I can put the deal together and make it work.

When you're selling, people are greedy and they want what they want. That's why when you're selling somebody, you have to have some means of takeaway from them. For example, recently I was having a conversation about a new invention where an individual had already put up about $25,000 in investment money. Nonchalantly, I told him, "You have $25,000 in this project and there's only so much stock available. Think about this. This is going to be a worldwide product that can make unbelievable amounts of money, so once the stock is sold, there is no more. You have the opportunity now to add to your $25,000 or to your shares of stock. Why not do that now before it's all gone?"

Finding project investors is really pretty simple because there is no shortage of them. All you need is a track record and a few successful projects that are so profitable that investors would be foolish not to work with you.

Allow me to give you an example. I was working on securing the funding for a warehousing project with another investor. His plan was to raise the money to be able to start building so he could sell it. I told him, "Look, why don't you have your plans. Let's go sell it first and then let's walk into the bank and build it. Let's do it on a pre-sale basis." He thought that was a good idea, and you might think the same thing too. If it's a project in which you can do pre-sales, such as a condominium project, then do it.

IV

TOOLS FOR SUCCESS

CHAPTER 16

CONTRACT TERMS

A win-win deal means that the project is priced so you can afford to sell your resulting product. But the most important thing really is the terms of your contract. You must have time built into your contract. Lots of folks want cash up front for their property, but you should be hesitant in buying property with no due diligence period. Look for a seller who is willing to give you the time. I'm not talking about free time. You only need a short period of free time, called due diligence or feasibility study period, to make sure you can successfully use the property exactly the way you want to use it and that there's a market for your use. I make sure all of my contracts contain reasonable due diligence periods.

The definition of reasonable depends on what you're going to build. Most condominium projects reasonably require six months. Once I get a free six-month lock, with a refundable deposit in escrow, I usually put down a larger deposit that's nonrefundable to extend the option to purchase for an additional 24 months while also making monthly payments. All of the deposits and monthly payments should apply to the purchase price.

Then, if you need another unit, you put up another substantial deposit and you continue making the payments. These deposits are refundable, so your landowners are protected and making money. Yet, if you were to buy a million-dollar piece of land, figure out what your payments are just on interest. Usually you're better off to just pay it directly to the landowner without making that loan.

When securing the funding, I recognize that I am usually cash poor, because I have my money invested and I don't like to borrow money to invest. So other than the construction loan or end loan, I don't like to borrow the initial funds that I need to put down because that is a risk.

The following is an actual contract on one of my condominium properties.

OPTION TO PURCHASE

THIS OPTION ("Option") is given this _____ day of_____,20_____, by_____, a Florida limited liability company, whose address is_____(the "Optionor"),to _____ a Florida limited liability company, whose address is _____ (the "Optionee").

1) Grant of Option. Optionor, in consideration of $10.00 paid by Optionee to Optionor, the receipt and sufficiency of which is acknowledged, grants to Optionee the exclusive right and option to purchase, on the following conditions, the real property in_____, which consists of the property as more fully described on Exhibit A attached and made a part hereof (the "Property"). This Option shall include all related water and sewer taps, but shall not include any furniture, fixtures, inventory or equipment located on or used in connection with the Property.

2) Option Period. The term of this Option shall commence upon the date the last party executes this Option ("Effective Date") and continue until _____p.m. on _____, ____ ("Option Period"), unless extended as provided herein.

3) Cost of Option. On the Effective Date (the "Due Date"), Optionee shall pay to_____, P.A.

163

("Escrow Agent") a deposit in the amount of Ten Thousand and no/100 Dollars ($10,000) in cash or in the form of a Letter of Credit (the "Option Payment"). Should Optionee not deliver the Option Payment to Escrow Agent by midnight on the Due Date, this Option shall become null and void and the parties shall be released from any and all obligations herein. At any time during the Option Period, Optionee may substitute the Option Payment if made in cash, with a Letter of Credit, at which time the cash shall be immediately returned to Optionee. In the event Optionee elects to terminate this Option within sixty (60) days from the Effective Date (the "Inspection Period"), the Escrow Agent shall return the Option Payment to the Optionee and this Option shall become null and void and the parties shall be released from any and all obligations herein. In the event Optionee does not terminate this Option within the Inspection Period, the Option Payment shall thereafter be non-refundable for any reason and shall be paid to Optionor by Escrow Agent upon the expiration of the Inspection Period. Should Optionee close on the transaction contemplated herein, the Option Payment shall be applied to reduce the Purchase Price.

4) Exercise of Option. Optionee shall exercise this Option by giving Optionor signed written notice no later than sixty (60) days before the Option Period or any extension thereof expires.

5) Extensions of Option Period. Optionee may extend the Option Period by Three Hundred and Sixty Five (365) days

("Extended Option Period") by notifying Optionor of its intent to extend the Option Period prior to the expiration of the Option Period, and by paying the Optionor the sum of Fifteen Thousand and no/100Dollars ($15,000), (the "Additional Option Payment") directly to Optionor prior to the expiration of the Option Period. The Additional Option Payment shall not be refundable for any reason and shall apply to the Purchase Price. Additionally, commencing on May 15, 2002, Optionee shall pay the sum of Fifteen Thousand andno/100 Dollars ($15,000) ("Monthly Extension Payments") per month directly to Optionor. The Monthly Extension Payments shall be due on the 15 'h day of each month, in advance ("Payment Date"). The Monthly Extension Payments shall not be refundable for any reason and shall apply to the Purchase Price.

At the end of the Extended Option Period, the Optionee may extend the Extended Option Period by an additional three hundred and sixty five (365) days ("Second Extended Option Period") giving the Optionor written notice of Optionee's intent to extend the Option Period prior to the expiration of the Extended Option Period and by paying the sum of and no/100 Dollars ($_____) ("Second Additional Option Payment") directly to Optionor prior to the expiration of the Extended Option Period. The Second Additional Option Payment shall not be refundable and shall apply to the Purchase Price. In addition to the Second Additional Option Payment, Optionee shall make monthly interest payments on the balance of the Purchase Price at _____percent (percent) APR (the "Interest Payments"). Interest Payments shall become due and payable on the Payment Date of the month following the commencement of the Second Extended Option Period and shall be due and payable each month thereafter by the Payment Date. The Interest Payments shall not be refundable and shall not apply to the Purchase Price.

The parties agree to negotiate in good faith for an additional three (3) month extension of this Option beyond the Second Additional Option Period if required by Optionee.

6) Terms of Agreement for Sale. Upon the exercise of this Option, the terms of the agreement for sale shall be as follows:

(a) Purchase Price. The purchase price of the Property is_____and no/100 Dollars. ("Purchase Price").

CHAPTER 17
FORMS AND CONTRACTS

The following list is provided for informational purposes only. Jerry Wallace Developments, LLC, is not responsible for the forms' content or reliability. Please consult your attorney prior to their use.

Legal Forms

The Website *www.accesslegalforms.com* offers more than 25,000 low-cost United States forms and documents you can download.

Landlord and Tenant Forms

(*www.accesslegalforms.com/landlord_tenant_ forms.htm*) Includes state-specific rental applications, notices, lease and sublease agreements, lead paint disclosure forms, closing documents, and much more.

Lease Agreements, Commercial

(*www.accesslegalforms.com/real_estate/commercial_ lease_forms.htm*) State-specific commercial leases, notices, forms, and agreements.

Lease Agreements, Residential

(*www.accesslegalforms.com/real_estate/residential_ lease_forms.htm*) State-specific residential leases and related documents.

Mortgages and Loan Forms

(*www.accesslegalforms.com/Mortgage_Loan_ Forms.htm*) State-specific forms, contracts, and agreements related to mortgages, loans, and deeds.

Options to Lease

(*www.accesslegalforms.com/real_estate/option_ to_lease_forms.htm*) State-specific residential and real estate forms and agreements related to optional lease and purchase.

Real Estate Closing Documents

(*www.accesslegalforms.com/real_estate/real_ estate_closing_forms.htm*) State-specific affidavits and other closing forms.

Real Estate Contracts

(*www.accesslegalforms.com/real_estate/real_ estate_contracts.htm*) Many residential and commercial real estate contracts, addendums, and other forms.

Real Estate Purchase

(*www.accesslegalforms.com/real_estate/real_ estate_purchase_sale_forms.htm*) State-specific real estate home sales packages.

Real Estate Law and Legal Resources

FindLaw

(*www.findlaw.com*) Extensive legal resources on the Web.

Cornell Law School

(*www.law.cornell.edu*) Valuable resource covering all aspects of law, including constitutions and codes, court opinions, law by source or jurisdiction, and much more.

Land-Use Law

(*www.law.cornell.edu/topics/land_use.html*) A brief overview of land-use law and an extensive menu of other available resources on the topic.

The 2005 Code of Ethics and Standards of Practice of the National Association of REALTORS®

(*www.realtor.org/mempolweb.nsf/pages/code*) Delineates Realtors' duties to clients and customers, the public, and other Realtors.

The Expropriation Law Centre

(*www.expropriationlaw.ca*) Known in the United States as "eminent domain," this site offers useful information on expropriation issues and legislation, including case law, news, articles, case reviews, and comments and statistics.

Foreclosure Process

(*http:foreclosure.searchking.com/foreclosure/information/foreclosure-process.htm*) State-specific explanations of foreclosure process and procedures.

Tax-Deferred Exchanges

(*www.wave.net/immigration/lawyer/tax_avoid.html*) A relatively brief and easy-to-understand guide to tax deferred exchanges.

Mexican Law Governing Real Estate

(*www.ricardobarraza.com/legal.html*) Site covers many aspects of property ownership in Mexico.

Mexico Law Guide

(*www.loc.gov/law/guide/mexico.html*) Law Library of Congress site featuring many issues regarding Mexican law.

Canadian Real Estate Law

(*www.canadalegal.com*) Find information through links to sites about Canadian laws relating to condominiums, commercial and residential real estate, and mortgages.

State Statutes and Legislation on the Internet

(*www.prairienet.org/~scruffy/f.htm*) Links to relevant state government sites, including state constitutions, statutes, and legislation.

State Statutes on Real Property

(*www.law.cornell.edu/topics/state_statutes.html*) An extensive topical index of a variety of state statutes.

U.S. State Constitutions, Statutes, Laws, and Codes

(*www.law.cornell.edu/statutes.html*)

Municipal Codes Online

(*www.spl.org/default.asp?pageID=collection _municodes*) Links to many municipalities' and counties' codes and ordinances, as well as links to code publishers.

U.S. Municipal Codes

(*www.municode.com*) A database of more municipal codes for more than 1,500 city and county governments listed by state.

Real Estate Legal Survival

(*www.legalsurvival.com/Real_Estate/*) Briefs on legal topics and case law.

Landlord Legal Survival

(*www.legalsurvival.com/Landlord_and_Tenant/*) Briefs on recent developments in case law and legal topics related to landlord and tenant issues.

Landlord Tenant Law

(*www.cses.com/rental/ltlaw.htm*) Generic and regionalized laws governing landlord and tenant relations.

Bankruptcy Questions

(*www.lectlaw.com/files/bnk06.htm*) Easy-to-understand answers to FAQs about bankruptcy

Real Estate Tools

Mortgage Amortization Calculator

(*www.hsh.com/calc-amort.html*) Use to create a monthly or yearly amortization schedule for a U.S. mortgage.

Construction Costs

(*www.get-a-quote.net*) Labor and material cost estimates for construction, including calculators to estimate material and supply quantities.

Office Space Calculator

(*www.officefinder.com/space_info.html*) Determines office space needs in usable square footage.

Commercial Mortgage Refinance Calculator

(*www.commercialmortgageyes.com*) Offers an evaluation of the benefits or costs of refinancing a mortgage loan.

CHAPTER 18

GENERAL ESCROW PROCEDURES FROM AROUND THE UNITED STATES

This summary is merely a general reference guide. Contact a local title company or real estate attorney for specific information. This guide is not offered as legal advice nor is it intended to be definitive. The author has included it as a general reference. These rules are constantly revised and due to this fact may no longer be accurate. Always consult with your attorney or broker for the latest legal procedures.

ALABAMA

Attorneys and title companies handle closings. Conveyance is by warranty deed. Mortgages are the customary security instruments. Foreclosures are nonjudicial. Foreclosure notices are published once a week for three weeks on a county-by-county basis. The foreclosure process takes a minimum of 21 days from the date of first publication. After the sale, there is a one-year redemption period. Alabamans use American Land Title Association (ALTA) policies to insure titles. Buyers and sellers negotiate who is going to pay the closing costs and usually split them equally. Property taxes are due and payable annually on October 1st.

ALASKA

Title companies, lenders, and private escrow companies all handle real estate escrows. Conveyance is by warranty deed. Deeds of trust with private power of sale are the customary security instruments. Foreclosures take 90–120 days. Alaskans use ALTA owner's and lender's policies with standard endorsements. There are no documentary or transfer taxes. Buyer and seller usually split the closing costs. Property tax payment dates vary throughout the state.

ARIZONA

Title companies and title agents both handle closings. Conveyance is by warranty deed. Whereas deeds of trust are the security instruments most often used, mortgages and "agreements for sale" are used approximately 20 percent of the time. Foreclosure depends on the security instrument. For deeds of trust, the foreclosure process takes about 91 days. Arizonans use ALTA owner's and lender's policies, standard or extended, with standard endorsements. The seller customarily pays for the owner's policy, and the buyer pays for the lender's policy. They split escrow costs otherwise. There are no documentary, transfer, or mortgage taxes. The first property tax installment is due October 1st and delinquent November 1st; the second half is due March 1st and delinquent May 1st. Arizona is a community-property state.

ARKANSAS

Title agents handle escrows, and attorneys conduct closings. Conveyance is by warranty deed. Mortgages are the customary security instruments. Foreclosure requires judicial proceedings, but there are no minimum time limits for completion. Arkansans use ALTA policies and endorsements and receive a 40 percent discount for reissuance of prior policies. Buyers and sellers pay their own escrow costs. The buyer pays for the lender's policy; the seller pays for the owner's. The buyer and seller split the state documentary tax. Property taxes come due three times a year as follows: the third Monday in April, the third Monday in July, and the 10th day of October.

CALIFORNIA

Not only do escrow procedures differ between Northern and Southern California, they also vary somewhat from county to county. Title companies handle closings through escrow in Northern California, whereas escrow companies and lenders handle them in Southern California. Conveyance is by grant deed. Deeds of trust with private power of sale are the security instruments used throughout the state. Foreclosure requires a three-month waiting period after the recording of the notice of default. After the waiting period, the notice of sale is published each week for three consecutive weeks. The borrower may reinstate the loan at any time prior to five business days before the foreclosure sale. All in all, the procedure takes about four months. Californians have both ALTA and California Land Title Association (CLTA) policies available. In Southern California, sellers pay the title insurance premium and the transfer tax. Buyer and seller split the escrow costs. In the Northern California counties of Amador, Merced, Plumas, San Joaquin, and Siskiyou, buyers and sellers share title insurance and escrow costs equally. In Butte County, sellers pay 75 percent; buyers pay 25 percent. In Alameda, Calaveras, Colusa, Contra Costa, Lake, Marin, Mendocino, San Francisco, San Mateo, Solano, and Sonoma counties, buyers pay for the title insurance policy, whereas sellers pay in the other Northern California counties. Each California county has its own transfer tax; some cities have additional charges. Property taxes may be paid annually on or before December 10th, or semiannually by December 10th and April 10th. California is a community-property state.

COLORADO

Title companies, brokers, and attorneys all may handle closings. Conveyance is by warranty deed. Deeds of trust are the customary security instruments. Public trustees must sell foreclosure properties within 45–60 days after the filing of a notice of election and demand for sale, but they will grant extensions up to six months following the date of the originally scheduled sale. Subdivided properties may be redeemed within 75 days after sale; agricultural properties may be redeemed within six months after sale. The first junior lienholder has 10 additional days to redeem, and the second and other junior lienholders have an additional five days each. The public trustee is normally the trustee shown on the deed of trust, a practice unique to Colorado. Foreclosures may be handled judicially. Coloradans have these title insurance policy options: ALTA owner's, lender's, leasehold, and construction loan; endorsements are used, too. Closing costs are generally split between the buyer and seller. The seller traditionally pays for the owner's title insurance premium and the documentary transfer tax. Property taxes may be paid annually at the end of April or semiannually at the ends of February and July.

CONNECTICUT

Attorneys normally conduct closings. Most often, conveyance is by warranty deed, but quitclaim deeds do appear. Mortgages are the security instruments. Judicial foreclosures are the rule, either by a suit in equity for strict foreclosure

177

or by a court decree of sale. Court decreed sales preclude redemption, but strict foreclosures allow redemption for three to six months, depending on the discretion of the court. There are lender's and owner's title insurance policies available with various endorsements. Buyers customarily pay for examination and title insurance, while sellers pay the documentary and conveyance taxes. Property tax payment dates vary by town.

DELAWARE

Attorneys handle closings. Although quitclaim and general warranty deeds are sometimes used, most conveyances are by special warranty deeds. Mortgages are the security instruments. Foreclosures are judicial and require 90–120 days to complete. ALTA policies and endorsements are prevalent. Buyers pay closing costs and the owner's title insurance premiums. Buyers and sellers share the state transfer tax. Property taxes are on an annual basis and vary by county.

DISTRICT OF COLUMBIA

Attorneys, title insurance companies, or their agents may conduct closings. Conveyances are by bargain-and-sale deeds. Though mortgages are available, the deed of trust, containing private power of sale, is the security instrument of choice. Foreclosures require at least six weeks and start with a 30-day notice of sale sent by certified mail. ALTA policies and endorsements insure title. Buyers generally pay closing costs, title insurance premiums, and recording taxes.

Sellers pay the transfer tax. Property taxes fall due annually or, if they're less than $100,000, semiannually, on September 15th and March 31st.

FLORIDA

Title companies and attorneys handle closings. Conveyance is by warranty deed. Mortgages are the customary security instruments. Foreclosures are judicial and take about three months. They involve service by the sheriff, a judgment of foreclosure and sale, advertising, public sale, and finally issuance of a certificate of sale and certificate of title. ALTA policies are commonplace. Buyers pay the escrow and closing costs, while county custom determines who pays for the title insurance. Sellers pay the documentary tax. Property taxes are payable annually, but the due and delinquent dates are months apart, November 1st and April 1st.

GEORGIA

Attorneys generally take care of closings. Conveyance is by warranty deed. Security deeds are the security instruments. Foreclosures are nonjudicial and take little more than a month because there's a power of attorney right in the security deed. Foreclosure advertising must appear for four consecutive weeks prior to the first Tuesday of the month; that's when foreclosure sales take place. Georgians use ALTA title insurance policies, including owner's and lender's, and they

179

use binders and endorsements. Buyers pay title insurance premiums and also closing costs usually. Sellers pay transfer taxes. Property tax payment dates vary across the state.

HAWAII

By law, only attorneys may prepare property transfer documents, but there are title and escrow companies available to handle escrows and escrow instructions. Conveyance of fee-simple property is by warranty deed; conveyance of leasehold property, which is common throughout the state, is by assignment of lease. Condominiums are everywhere in Hawaii and may be fee simple or leasehold. Sales of some properties, whether fee simple or leasehold, are by agreement of sale. Mortgages are the security instruments. Hawaiians use judicial foreclosures rather than powers of sale for both mortgages and agreements of sale. These foreclosures take six to12 months and sometimes more, depending on court schedules. Title companies issue ALTA owner's and lender's policies and make numerous endorsements available. Buyers and sellers split escrow fees. Sellers pay the title search costs and the conveyance tax. Buyers pay title insurance premiums for the owner's and lender's policies. Property taxes come due twice a year, on February 20th and August 20th.

IDAHO

Closings are handled through escrow. Conveyance is by warranty deed or corporate deed, though often there are contracts of sale involved. Either mortgages or deeds of trust may be the security instruments. Deeds of trust that include power of sale provisions are restricted to properties in incorporated areas and properties elsewhere that don't exceed 20 acres. After the notice of default has been recorded, deed-of-trust foreclosures take at least 120 days, and there's no redemption period. Judicial foreclosures for mortgages take about a year, depending on court availability, and there's a six to 12 month redemption period after that, depending on the type of property involved. Idahoans use ALTA policies and various endorsements. Buyers and sellers split escrow costs in general and negotiate who's going to pay the title insurance premiums. There are no documentary taxes, mortgage taxes, or transfer taxes, but there are property taxes, and they're due annually in November and delinquent on December 20th, or semiannually on December 20th and June 20th. Idaho is a community-property state.

ILLINOIS

Title companies, lenders, and attorneys may conduct closings, but only attorneys may prepare documents. Lenders generally hire attorneys and have them prepare all the paperwork. Conveyance is by warranty deed. Recorded deeds must include a declaration of the sales price. Mortgages are the customary security instruments. Judicial foreclosure is mandatory and takes at least a year from the filing of the default notice to the expiration of the redemption period. Illinoisans use ALTA policies. Buyers usually pay the closing costs and the lender's title insurance premiums; sellers pay the owner's title insurance premiums and the state and county transfer taxes. Property tax payment dates vary. Larger counties typically schedule them for March 1st and September 1st, and smaller counties schedule them for June 1st and September 1st.

INDIANA

Title companies, lenders, real estate agents, and attorneys handle closings. Conveyance is by warranty deed. Mortgages are the customary security instruments. Judicial foreclosures are required; execution of judgments varies from three months after filing of the complaint in cases involving mortgages drawn up since July 1, 1975, to six months for those drawn up between January 1, 1958, and July 1, 1975, to 12 months for those drawn up before that. Immediately following the execution sale, the highest bidder receives a sheriff's deed. Hoosiers use ALTA policies and certain endorsements. Buyers usually pay closing costs and the lender's title insurance costs, while sellers pay for the owner's policy. There are no documentary, mortgage, or transfer taxes. Property taxes fall due on May 10th and November 10th.

IOWA

Attorneys may conduct closings, and so may real estate agents. Conveyance is usually by warranty deed. Mortgages and deeds of trust are both authorized security instruments, but lenders prefer mortgages because deeds of trust do not circumvent judicial foreclosure proceedings anyway. Those proceedings take at least four to six months. Because Iowa is the only state that does not authorize title insurance, Iowans who want it must go through a title company in another state. Buyers and sellers share the closing costs; sellers pay the documentary taxes. Property taxes are due July 1st based on the previous January's assessment.

KANSAS

Title companies, lenders, real estate agents, attorneys, and independent escrow firms all conduct closings. Anyone who conducts a title search must be a licensed abstracter, a designation one receives after passing strict tests and meeting various requirements. Because many land titles stem from Indian origins, deeds involving Indians as parties to a transaction go before the Indian Commission for approval. Conveyance is by warranty deed. Mortgages are the customary security instruments. Judicial foreclosures, the only ones allowed, take about six months from filing to sale. Redemption periods vary, the longest being 12 months. Kansans use ALTA policies and endorsements. Buyers and sellers divide closing costs. Buyers pay the lender's policy costs and the state mortgage taxes; sellers pay for the owner's policy. Property taxes come due November 1st, but they needn't be paid in a lump sum until December 31st. They may also be paid in two installments, the first on December 20th and the second on June 20th.

KENTUCKY

Attorneys conduct closings. Conveyance is by grant deed or by bargain-and-sale deed. Deeds must show the name of the preparer, the amount of the total transaction, and the recording reference by which the grantor obtained title. Mortgages are the principal security instruments because deeds of trust offer no power-of-sale advantages. Enforcement of any security instrument requires a decree in equity, a judicial foreclosure proceeding. Kentuckians use ALTA policies and endorsements. Sellers pay closing costs; buyers pay recording fees. Responsibility for payment of title insurance premiums varies according to locale. Property taxes are payable on an annual basis; due dates vary from county to county.

LOUISIANA

Either attorneys or corporate title agents may conduct closings, but a notary must authenticate the documentation. Conveyance is by warranty deed or by act of sale. Mortgages are the security instruments generally used in commercial transactions, while vendor's liens and seller's privileges are used in other purchase money situations. Foreclosures are swift (60 days) and sure (no right of redemption). Successful foreclosure sale bidders receive an adjudication from the sheriff. Louisianians use ALTA owner's and lender's policies and endorsements. Buyers generally pay the title insurance and closing costs. There are no mortgage or transfer taxes. Property tax payment dates vary from parish to parish (parishes are like counties). Louisiana is a community-property state.

MAINE

Attorneys conduct closings. Conveyance is by warranty or quitclaim deed. Mortgages are the security instruments. Foreclosures may be initiated by any of the following: an act of law for possession; entering into possession and holding the premises by written consent of the mortgagor; entering peaceably, openly, and unopposed in the presence of two witnesses and taking possession; giving public notice in a newspaper for three successive weeks and recording copies of the notice in the Registry of Deeds, and then recording the mortgage within 30 days of the last publication; or by a bill in equity (special cases). In every case, the creditor must record a notice of foreclosure within 30 days. Judicial foreclosure proceedings are also available. Redemption periods vary from 90 to 365 days, depending on the method of foreclosure. Mainers use ALTA owner's and lender's policies and endorsements. Buyers pay closing costs and title insurance fees; buyers and sellers share the documentary transfer taxes. Property taxes are due annually on April 1st.

MARYLAND

Attorneys conduct closings, and there has to be a local attorney involved. Conveyance is by grant deed, and the deed must state the consideration involved. Although mortgages are common in some areas, deeds of trust are more prevalent as security instruments. Security instruments may include a private power of sale, so it naturally is the foreclosure method of choice. Marylanders use ALTA policies and endorsements. Buyers pay closing costs, title insurance premiums, and transfer taxes. Property taxes are due annually on July 1st.

MASSACHUSETTS

Attorneys handle closings. Conveyance is by warranty deed in the western part of the state and by quitclaim deed in the eastern part. Mortgages with private power of sale are the customary security instruments. Creditors forced to foreclose generally take advantage of the private power of sale, but they may foreclose through peaceable entry (entering unopposed in the presence of two witnesses and taking possession for three years) or through the rarely used judicial writ of entry. Frequently, cautious creditors will foreclose through both power of sale and peaceable entry. People in Massachusetts use ALTA owner's and lender's title insurance policies and endorsements. Buyers pay closing costs and title insurance fees, except in Worcester, where sellers pay. Sellers pay the documentary taxes. Property taxes are payable in two installments, November 1st and May 1st.

MICHIGAN

Title companies, lenders, real estate agents, and attorneys may conduct closings. Conveyance is by warranty deed, which must give the full consideration involved or be accompanied by an affidavit that does. Many transactions involve land contracts. Mortgages are the security instruments. Private foreclosure is permitted; it requires advertising for four consecutive weeks and a sale at least 28 days following the date of first publication. The redemption period ranges from one to 12 months. Michiganders use ALTA policies and endorsements. Buyers generally pay closing costs and the lender's title insurance premium, and sellers pay the state transfer tax and the owner's title insurance premium. Property taxes that pay for city and school expenses fall due July 1st; others (county taxes, township taxes, and some school taxes) fall due on the first of December. In many tax jurisdictions, taxpayers may opt to pay their taxes in two equal installments without penalty.

MINNESOTA

Title companies, lenders, real estate agents, and attorneys may conduct closings. Conveyance is by warranty deed. Although deeds of trust are authorized, mortgages are the customary security instruments. The redemption period following a foreclosure is six months in most cases; it is 12 months if the property is larger than 10 acres or the amount claimed to be due is less than 2/3 of the original debt. This is a strong abstract state. Typically, a buyer will accept an abstract and an attorney's opinion as evidence of title, even though the lender may require title insurance. People in the Minneapolis-St. Paul area use the Torrens system. Minnesotans use ALTA policies. Buyers pay the lender's and owner's title insurance premiums and the mortgage tax. Sellers usually pay the closing fees and the transfer taxes. Property taxes are due on May 15th and October 15th

MISSISSIPPI

Attorneys conduct real estate closings. Conveyance is by warranty deed. Deeds of trust are the customary security instruments. Foreclosure involves a nonjudicial process, which takes 21–45 days. Mississippians use ALTA policies and endorsements. Buyers and sellers negotiate the payment of title insurance premiums and closing costs. There are no documentary, mortgage, or transfer taxes. Property taxes are payable on an annual basis and become delinquent February 1st.

MISSOURI

Title companies, lenders, real estate agents, and attorneys may conduct closings. In the St. Louis area, title company closings predominate. In the Kansas City area, an escrow company or a title company generally conducts the closing. Conveyance is by warranty deed. Deeds of trust are the customary security instruments and allow private power of sale. The trustee must be named in the deed of trust and must be a Missouri resident. Foreclosure involves publication of a sale notice for 21 days, during which time the debtor may redeem the property or file a notice of redemption. The foreclosure sale buyer receives a trustee's deed. Missourians use ALTA policies and endorsements. Buyers and sellers generally split the closing costs. Sellers in western Missouri usually pay for the title insurance polices, while elsewhere the buyers pay. There are no documentary, mortgage, or transfer taxes. Property taxes are payable annually and become delinquent January 1st for the previous year.

MONTANA

Real estate closings are handled through escrow. Conveyance is by warranty deed, corporate deed, or grant deed. Mortgages, deeds of trust, and unrecorded contracts of sale are the security instruments. Mortgages require judicial foreclosure, and there's a six to12 month redemption period following sale. Foreclosure on deeds of trust involves filing a notice of default and then holding a trustee sale 120 days later. Montanans use ALTA policies and endorsements. Buyers and sellers split the escrow and closing costs; sellers usually pay for the title insurance policies. There are no documentary, mortgage, or transfer taxes. Montanans may pay their property taxes annually by November 30th or semi-annually by November 30th and May 31st.

NEBRASKA

Title companies, lenders, real estate agents, and attorneys all conduct closings. Conveyance is by warranty deed. Mortgages and deeds of trust are the security instruments. Mortgage foreclosures require judicial proceedings and take about six months from the date of the first notice when they're uncontested. Deeds of trust do not require judicial proceedings and take about 90 days. Nebraskans use ALTA policies and endorsements. Buyers and sellers split escrow and closing costs; sellers pay the state's documentary taxes. Property taxes fall due April 1st and August 1st.

NEVADA

Escrow similar to California's is used for closings. Conveyance is by grant deed, bargain-and-sale deed, or quitclaim deed. Deeds of trust are the customary security instruments. Foreclosure involves recording a notice of default and mailing a copy within 10 days. Following the mailing, there is a 35-day reinstatement period. After that, the beneficiary may accept partial payment or payment in full for a three-month period. Then come advertising the property for sale for three consecutive weeks and finally the sale itself. All of this takes about 4 1/2 months. Nevadans use both ALTA and CLTA policies and endorsements. Buyers and sellers share escrow costs. Buyers pay the lender's title insurance premiums; sellers pay the owner's and the state's transfer tax. Property taxes are payable in one, two, or four payments, the first one being due July 1st. Nevada is a community-property state.

NEW HAMPSHIRE

Attorneys conduct real estate closings. Conveyance is by warranty or quitclaim deed. Mortgages are the customary security instruments. Lenders may foreclosure through judicial action or through whatever power of sale was written into the mortgage originally. Entry, either by legal action or by taking possession peaceably in the presence of two witnesses, is possible under certain legally stated conditions. There is a one-year right-of-redemption period. The people of New Hampshire use ALTA owner's and lender's policies. Buyers pay all closing costs and title fees except for the documentary tax; that's shared with the sellers. Property tax payment dates vary across the state.

NEW JERSEY

Attorneys handle closings in northern New Jersey, and title agents customarily handle them elsewhere. Conveyance is by bargain-and-sale deed with covenants against grantors' acts (equivalent to a special warranty deed). Mortgages are the most common security instruments, though deeds of trust are authorized. Foreclosures require judicial action, which takes six to nine months if uncontested. New Jerseyites use ALTA owner's and lender's policies. Both buyer and seller pay the escrow and closing costs. The buyer pays the title insurance fees, and the seller pays the transfer tax. Property taxes are payable quarterly on the first of April, July, October, and January.

NEW MEXICO

Real estate closings are conducted through escrows. Conveyance is by warranty or quitclaim deed. Deeds of trust and mortgages are the security instruments. Foreclosures require judicial proceedings, and there's a nine-month redemption period after judgment. New Mexicans use ALTA owner's, lender's, and construction and leasehold policies; they also use endorsements. Buyers and sellers share escrow costs equally; sellers pay the title insurance premiums. There are no documentary, mortgage, or transfer taxes. Property taxes are payable November 5th and April 5th. New Mexico is a community-property state.

NEW YORK

All parties to a transaction appear with their attorneys for closing. Conveyance is by bargain-and-sale deed. Mortgages are the security instruments in this lien-theory state. Foreclosures require judicial action and take several months if uncontested or longer if contested. New Yorkers use policies of the New York Board of Title Underwriters almost exclusively, though some use the New York State 1946 ALTA Loan Policy. Buyers generally pay most closing costs, including all title insurance fees and mortgage taxes. Sellers pay the state and city transfer taxes. Property tax payment dates vary across the state.

NORTH CAROLINA

Attorneys or lenders may handle closings, and corporate agents issue title insurance. Conveyance is by warranty deed. Deeds of trust with private power of sale are the customary security instruments. Foreclosures are nonjudicial, with a 10-day redemption period following the sale. The entire process takes between 45 and 60 days. North Carolinians use ALTA policies, but these require an attorney's opinion before they're issued. Buyers and sellers negotiate the closing costs, except that buyers pay the recording costs, and sellers pay the document preparation and transfer tax costs. Property taxes fall due annually on the last day of the year.

NORTH DAKOTA

Lenders, together with attorneys, conduct closings. Conveyance is by warranty deed. Mortgages are the security instruments. Foreclosures require about six months, including the redemption period. North Dakotans base their title insurance on abstracts and attorneys' opinions. Buyers usually pay for the closing, the attorney's opinion, and the title insurance; sellers pay for the abstract. There are no documentary or transfer taxes. Property taxes are due March 15th and October 15th.

OHIO

Title companies and lenders hanJle closings. Conveyance is by warranty deed. Dower rights require that all documents involving a married person must be executed by both spouses. Mortgages are the security instruments. Judicial foreclosures, the only kind allowed, require about six to12 months. People in Ohio use ALTA policies; they get a commitment at closing and a policy following the recording of documents. Buyers and sellers negotiate who's going to pay closing costs and title insurance premiums, but sellers pay the transfer taxes. Property tax payment dates vary throughout the state.

OKLAHOMA

Title companies, lenders, real estate agents, and attorneys may conduct closings. Conveyance is by warranty deed. Mortgages are the usual security instruments. Foreclosures may be by judicial action or by power of sale if properly allowed for in the security instrument. Oklahomans use ALTA policies and endorsements. Buyers and sellers share the closing costs, except that the buyer pays the lender's policy premium, the seller pays the documentary transfer tax, and the lender pays the mortgage tax. Property taxes may be paid annually on or before the last day of the year, or semi-annually by December 31st and March 31st.

OREGON

Closings are handled through escrow. Conveyance is by warranty or bargain-and-sale deed, but land sales contracts are common. Mortgage deeds and deeds of trust are the security instruments. Oregon attorneys usually act as trustees in nonjudicial trust-deed foreclosures. Such foreclosures take five months from the date of the sale notice; defaults may be cured as late as five days prior to sale. Judicial foreclosures on either mortgages or trust deeds allow for a one-year redemption period following sale. Oregonians use ALTA and Oregon Land Title Association policies. Buyers and sellers split escrow costs and transfer taxes; the buyer pays for the lender's title insurance policy, and the seller pays for the owner's policy. Property taxes are payable the 15th of November, February, and May; if paid in full by November 15th, owners receive a 3 percent reduction.

PENNSYLVANIA

Title companies, real estate agents, and approved attorneys may handle closings. Conveyance is by special or general warranty deed. Mortgages are the security instruments. Foreclosures take one to six months from filing through judgment plus another two months or more from judgment through sale. State law restricts aliens in owning real property with respect to acreage and income and includes special restrictions affecting farmland. Pennsylvanians use ALTA owner's, lender's, and leasehold policies. Buyers pay closing costs and title insurance fees; buyers and sellers split the transfer taxes. Property tax payment dates differ across the state.

RHODE ISLAND

Attorneys usually conduct closings, but banks and title companies may also conduct them. Conveyance is by warranty or quitclaim deed. Mortgages are the usual security instruments. Foreclosures follow the power-of-sale provisions contained in mortgage agreements and take about 45 days. Power-of-sale foreclosures offer no redemption provisions, whereas any other foreclosure method carries a three-year right of redemption. Rhode Islanders use ALTA policies and endorsements. Buyers pay title insurance premiums and closing costs; sellers pay documentary taxes. Property taxes are payable annually, semi-annually, or quarterly with the first payment due in July.

SOUTH CAROLINA

Attorneys customarily handle closings. Conveyance is by warranty deed. Mortgages are most often the security instruments. Foreclosures are judicial and take three to five months, depending on court schedules. Foreclosure sales take place on the first Monday of every month following publication of notice once a week for three consecutive weeks. South Carolinians use owner's and lender's ALTA policies and endorsements. Buyers pay closing costs, title insurance premiums, and state mortgage taxes; sellers pay the transfer taxes.

Property tax payment dates vary across the state from September 15 to December 31.

SOUTH DAKOTA

Title companies, lenders, real estate agents, and attorneys may handle closings. Conveyance is by warranty deed. Mortgages are the usual security instruments. Foreclosures may occur through judicial proceedings or through the power-of-sale provisions contained in certain mortgage agreements. Sheriff's sales follow publication of notice by 30 days. The redemption period allowed after sale of parcels smaller than 40 acres and encumbered by mortgages containing power of sale is 180 days; in all other cases, it's a year. There's a unique statute that stipulates that all land must be platted in lots or described by sectional references rather than by metes and bounds unless it involves property described in documents recorded prior to 1945. There's another unique statute called the Affidavit of Possession Statute. Certain exceptions aside, it provides that any person having an unbroken chain of title for 22 years thereafter has a marketable title free of any defects occurring prior to that 22-year period. South Dakotans use ALTA policies and endorsements. Sellers pay the transfer taxes and split the other closing costs, fees, and premiums with the buyers. Property taxes come due May 1st and November 1st

TENNESSEE

A title company attorney, a party to the contract, a lender's representative, or an outside attorney may conduct a closing. Conveyance is by warranty or quitclaim deed. Deeds of trust are the customary security instruments. Foreclosures, which are handled according to trustee sale provisions, are swift, that is, 22 days from the first publication of the notice until the public sale, and there is normally no right of redemption after that. Tennesseans use ALTA policies and endorsements. The payment of title insurance premiums, closing costs, mortgage taxes, and transfer taxes varies according to local practice. Property taxes are payable annually on the first Monday in October.

TEXAS

Title companies normally handle closings. Conveyance is by warranty deed. Deeds of trust are the most common security instruments. Following the posting of foreclosure sales at the local courthouse for at least 21 days, the sales themselves take place at the courthouse on the first Tuesday of the month. Texans use only Texas standard policy forms of title insurance. Buyers and sellers negotiate closing costs. There aren't any documentary, transfer, or mortgage taxes. Property taxes are due October 1st. Texas is a community-property state.

UTAH

Lenders handle about 60 percent of the escrows and title companies handle the rest. Conveyance is by warranty deed. Mortgages and deeds of trust with private power of sale are the security instruments. Mortgage foreclosures require judicial proceedings, which take about a year; deed-of-trust foreclosures take advantage of private power-of-sale provisions and take about four months. Utahans use ALTA owner's and lender's policies and endorsements. Buyers and sellers split escrow fees, and sellers pay the title insurance premiums. There are no documentary, transfer, or mortgage taxes. Property taxes are payable November 30th.

VERMONT

Attorneys take care of closings. Conveyance is by warranty or quitclaim deed. Mortgages are the customary security instruments, but large commercial transactions often employ deeds of trust. Mortgage foreclosures require judicial proceedings for strict foreclosure; after sale, there is a redemption period of one year for mortgages dated prior to April 1, 1968, and six months for all others. Vermonters use ALTA owner's and lender's policies and endorsements. Buyers pay recording fees, title insurance premiums, and transfer taxes. Property tax payment dates vary across the state.

VIRGINIA

Attorneys and title companies conduct real estate closings. Conveyance is by bargain-and-sale deed. Deeds of trust are the customary security instruments. Foreclosure takes about two months. Virginians use ALTA policies and endorsements. Buyers pay the title insurance premiums and the various taxes. Property tax payment dates vary.

WASHINGTON

Title companies, independent escrow companies, lenders, and attorneys may handle escrows. An attorney must prepare real estate documents, but there is a limited practice rule that lets licensed non-attorneys prepare most of the commonly used real estate documents. Conveyance is by warranty deed. Both deeds of trust with private power of sale and mortgages are used as security instruments. Mortgages require judicial foreclosure. Deeds of trust require that a notice of default be sent first, and, 30 days later, a notice of sale. The notice of sale must be recorded, posted, and mailed at least 90 days before the sale, and the sale cannot take place any earlier than 190 days after the actual default. Sellers generally pay the title insurance premiums and the revenue tax; buyers and sellers split everything else. Property taxes are payable April 30th and October 31st. Washington is a community-property state.

WEST VIRGINIA

Attorneys conduct escrow closings, although lenders and real estate agents do them occasionally. Conveyance is by warranty deed, bargain-and-sale deed, or grant deed. Deeds of trust are the customary security instruments. Foreclosures are great for lenders; when uncontested, they take only a month. West Virginians use ALTA policies and endorsements. Buyers pay the title insurance premiums and sellers pay the documentary taxes; they divide the other closing costs. Property taxes may be paid in a lump sum after July 6th or in two installments on September 1st and March 1st.

WISCONSIN

Lenders and title companies conduct what are called "table closings" throughout the state, except in the Milwaukee area, where attorneys conduct the closings. Conveyance is by warranty deed, but installment land contracts are used extensively, too. Mortgages are the customary security instruments. Within limits, the actual mortgage wording determines foreclosure requirements; redemption varies from two months for abandoned property to a full year in some cases. Lenders generally waive their right to a deficiency judgment in order to reduce the redemption period to six months. Wisconsinites use ALTA policies and endorsements. Buyers generally pay closing costs and the lender's policy fees; sellers pay the owner's policy fees and the transfer taxes. In transactions involving homesteads, conveyances may be void if not joined into by the spouse. Property taxes may be paid in full on February 28th, or they may be paid half on January 31st and half on July 31st. Wisconsin is a quasi-community-property state.

WYOMING

Real estate agents generally conduct closings. Conveyance is by warranty deed. Mortgages are the usual security instruments. Foreclosures may follow judicial or power-of-sale proceedings. Residential foreclosures take around 120 days; agricultural foreclosures, around 13 months. Wyomingites use ALTA owner's and lender's policies and endorsements. Buyer and seller negotiate who's going to pay the various closing costs and title insurance fees. There are no documentary, mortgage, or transfer taxes. Property taxes may be paid annually December 31st or semi-annually September 1st and March 1st.

CHAPTER 19

CONCLUSION

Filmmaking legend Samuel Goldwyn once said, "The harder I work the luckier I get."

Like Goldwyn, many people have or had what is called luck, especially if they worked hard to get it! There are also people who were in the right place at the right time, including those who inherited money from their parents. But you cannot wait for luck! You must create your own luck by using your head, working hard, and remembering what makes a person successful in this world.

Here are some tips I've used throughout the years that can help you be successful.

1. Never make negative statements about your peers.

2. Never go back on your word, even if it is severely to your detriment.

3. Always pay your debts in full and on time.

4. Always be on time for appointments.

5. Never leave another partner/co-broker/agent thinking you didn't honor the agreement/commission amount you agreed upon.

6. Always get even your smallest agreements in writing and signed by both parties. This will prevent most conflicts.

To be successful, you need to surround yourself with the right people. You should avoid people who:

1. Cheat.

2. Lie.

3. Avoid paying their debts.

4. Have unhealthy addictions.

5. Cannot control their tempers.

6. Are unethical or suggest unethical actions.

Stick to these characteristics and you'll make it big in real estate.

Can it work for you? Yes it can.

How do I know? Because it worked for me.

RESOURCES

These are services that could assist you in your career as a power broker. They are provided for your perusal and convenience, but are not directly endorsed by the author.

Listing Services

• **Airport properties**
www.airportclassified.com For sale and lease.

• **Bed & Breakfast properties for sale**
www.bedandbreakfastforsale.com Directory of small lodging properties, hotels, and inns for sale.

• **Canadian Multiple Listing Services**
www.mls.ca MLS covering all provinces in Canada.

• **Commercial properties**
www.naidirect.com Office, retail, industrial, development properties, and apartment buildings.

• **Commercial properties for sale or lease**
www.barryinc.com/pbegin.cfm Land, office, industrial, and retail properties.

• **Commercial real estate**
www.commrex.com Search investment, commercial, and industrial property listings throughout the United States.

- **Farms and farmland**

www.landandfarm.com Search for land and farms for sale in the United States, Canada, and more than 200 other countries.

- **Lodgings**

www.hotelrealtyresource.com National and international listings of hotels, motels, inns, restaurants, and other properties for sale.

- **Hotels & motels FSBO**

www.hotels-fsbo.com Hotels, motels, B&B's, and other lodging establishments for sale by owner.

- **Investment real estate**

www.1031Properties.com Single-tenant net leased properties for sale.

- **Private islands**

www.privateislandsonline.com Directory of private islands for sale or rent.

- **Real estate exchange marketing**

www.RealEstateExchange.com A multiple listing service for the exchange or sale of commercial and investment property.

- **Resorts**

www.ResortsForSale.com On-line guide to resorts for sale in North America, featuring photos, descriptions, and contact information.

• **Retail space**

www.storetrax.com Real Estate listing service, provides contact information, and other valuable tools.

• **Retreat properties**

www.allaboutretreats.com Retreats, ranches, or resort properties available for redevelopment in North and Central America.

• **RV parks & campgrounds for sale**

www.rvparkstore.com/list.htm Assists in the selling or buying of RVs. Appraisals included.

Directories and Guides

• **Appraisers**

www.zipappraisers.com Find appraisers by state.

• **Appraisers**

www.AppraiserDatabase.com Search for appraisers by county.

• **Architecture firms**

www.architectsusa.com Searchable database of more than 20,000 architects.

• **Canadian Directory of Federal Real Property**

www.tbs-sct.gc.ca Central record and of property holdings of the Government of Canada.

- **Chamber of Commerce directory**

www.clickcity.com Search for resources by city or state.

- **Commercial realtors**

www.allre.com Search directory for agents, listings, and other real estate-related information.

- **CORFAC International**

www.corfac.com/PropertyListings.asp Property listings and other real estate services in United States, Canada, and Mexico.

- **Corporate information**

www.corporateinformation.com Search more than 300,000 company profiles worldwide and browse links to information on corporations categorized regionally.

- **County recorders**

www.zanatec.com/home.html List of United States county recorders, including addresses and phone numbers.

- **Economic development directory**

www.ecodevdirectory.com Directory of national and international economic development agencies, consultants, and associations.

- **Employment**

www.realestatejobstore.com Post your resume or find a real estate job listing.

- **Environmental databases (U.S.)**

www.epa.gov From the Environmental Protection Agency (EPA).

- **Environmental Pollution Directory**

www.scorecard.org Information on toxic chemical pollution throughout the United States by county.

- **Environmental professionals**

www.expertpages.com Find an environmental expert.

- **Hazardous sites**

www.epa.gov Locate hazardous waste sites.

- **Escrow and title service**

www.escrowandtitleservice.com Comprehensive directory of real estate escrow and title services in United States.

- **Foreclosures**

www.realestateforeclosures.com Daily updated database of real estate foreclosures in all states, including details, photos, and contact information

- **Lawyer locator**

www.lawyers.com All countries.

- **Legal database**

www.Lawoffice.com More than 400 legal topics and a directory of attorneys categorized by state and specialty.

- **Manufactured home communities**
www.mobilehomeparkstore.com Nationwide directory.

- **Mexican brokers and agents**
www.mexonline.com/reagents.htm Online guide to Mexico's Real estate agents.

- **Mortgage rates by state**
www.interest.com Shows National mortgage rates and provides refinancing tools.

- **Municipal codes**
www.spl.org/default.asp?pageID= collection_municodes Links to many municipalities' and counties' codes and ordinances, as well as links to code publishers.

- **National Register of Historic Places**
www.nr.nps.gov Database of listed properties.

- **Official city sites: Canada**
www.officialcitysites.org/canada.php3 Links to officially sanctioned city, county, area, regional, and state Websites and information.

- **Official city sites: U.S.**
www.officialcitysites.org Links to officially sanctioned city, county, area, regional, and state Websites and information.

• **Outlet stores and centers**

www.outletbound.com Includes links for developers and retailers.

• **Property managers**

www.us-management.com Search database for accredited property managers by city and state.

• **Real estate agents**

www.allre.com Search for an agent by state and by specialty.

• **Real estate auctioneers**

www.realtycentral.com/auction/link1.htm Links to auctioneers' sites.

• **Real estate auctions**

www.internetauctionlist.com Provides an up-to-date auction list on real estate.

• **Real estate clubs**

www.creonline.com/real-estate-clubs/index.html Directory of real estate clubs listed by state.

• **Real estate investment trusts**

www.inrealty.com Institutional and commercial real estate investment information.

• **Retail real estate**

www.PlainVanillaShell.com Information and resources for the retail real estate industry.

- **Shopping malls**
www.icsc.org/me/directories.php A directory of major U.S. shopping centers.

- **Skyscrapers**
www.skyscrapers.com Resource for information on high-rises worldwide.

- **Surveying companies**
www.lsrp.com Directory of surveyors by state.

- **Tax assessor database**
www.pubweb.acns.nwu.edu Searchable by state and includes links to assessors' Websites when available.

- **Retail industry data**
www.retailindustry.about.com/ Online service for retail chain-store executives.

- **Office buildings directory**
www.mrofficespace.com Provides a list of office buildings in 11 major cities.

Real Estate News

- **Canada NewsWire**
www.newswire.ca/htmindex/industry.htm News releases by industry.

- **Chain Store Age**

www.chainstoreage.com Resource for retail executives.

- **Commercial property news**

www.commercialpropertynews.com/cpn/index.jsp News and analysis of major property types and business areas.

- **CoStar Daily News**

www.costargroup.com Local news, statistics, and information for the United States commercial real estate industry.

- **Daily Mortgage News**

http://mortgages.interest.com/news.htm Provides daily updates on mortgage rates.

- **GlobeSt.com**

www.globest.com News and property resource guide.

- **Home Town News**

www.hometownnews.com Links to all known daily and weekly United States newspapers with Web sites.

- **Multi-Housing News**

www.multi-housingnews.com/multihousing/index.jsp News on affordable housing, luxury housing, property management, rehab, and finance.

- **National Mortgage News**

www.nationalmortgagenews.com Reports on the mortgage industry, including links to the major lenders and brokers.

- **Newspapers and news media**

www.abyznewslinks.com Links to news sources throughout the world.

- **Real Estate Journal**

www.realestatejournal.com Articles, news and real estate trends for the residential and commercial markets by the *Wall Street Journal.*

- **Shopping Center Today Newswire**

www.icsc.org The latest news on retail centers and shopping malls.

Journals and Publications

- **American Demographics Magazine**

www.adage.com/section.cms?sectionId=195 American demographics articles discussing mortgage rates and the market.

- **Builder Online Magazine**

www.builderonline.com. Homebuilding news, plans, and design ideas for home.

- **Building Design & Construction**

www.bdcnetwork.com Information for building owners and facility managers, architects, engineers, and contractors.

- **Constructech**

www.constructech.com Educates construction and facility management professionals about available technology.

- **Construction Journals and News**
www.constructioneducation.com/search/Construction_Journals_and_News Provides lists of construction journals and daily news.

- *Design Cost and Data*
www.dcd.com Cost-estimating magazine for architects, contractors, engineers, and others in the industry.

- *Development Magazine*
www.naiop.org/developmentmag Explores issues of interest to developers, owners, and managers of office and industrial properties.

- *Environmental Building News*
www.buildinggreen.com/ecommerce/ebn.cfm Newsletter on environmentally responsible design and construction.

- *Journal of Real Estate Finance and Economics*
www.jrefe.org A journal on the economics and finance of the real estate market.

- **Mortgage Daily**
www.mortgagedaily.com Daily news updates for mortgage professionals.

- **National Real Estate Investor Magazine**
www.nreionline.com Covers financing, investment, management, development, and leasing of commercial real estate.

- *Professional Surveyor Magazine*

www.profsurv.com Overview of professionals in mapping, surveying, and engineering.

- **Real Estate Portfolio**

www.nareit.com/portfoliomag/default.shtml For the REIT and publicly traded real estate industry.

- *Real Estate Professional*

www.therealestatepro.com Bimonthly magazine for real estate sales and management.

- *Realtor Magazine*

www.realtor.org/RealtorMag Business tools for real estate professionals.

- **REM Online**

www.remonline.com/rem/home.aspx Independent news and opinion for Canada's real estate industry.

- *Retail Traffic*

http://retailtrafficmag.com Shopping center and retail real estate magazine and current news.

- *Shopping Center Business*

www.shoppingcenterbusiness.com A business magazine over viewing the shopping center industry.

- **Site Remediation Technologies**

www.clu-in.org/remed1.cfm Descriptions, technology selection tools, programs, organizations, and publications.

Index

About the Author

"The Dealmaker," is a developer, entrepreneur, author, and one of the most publicized real estate professionals in America. Jerry Wallace's existing and proposed real estate developments over the past four years exceed $3 billion and his personal real estate sales volume exceed one billion. A graduate of the University of Alabama, he was recognized as the most successful pre-construction developer and real estate agent in the entire southeastern United States. He not only has a trademarked cocktail that bears his name—"The Dealmaker"—but is owner of an entire township in Texas, "Wallace Town USA," something no one else in the country can boast. Jerry Walace is a consummate trend setter in the development and real estate buisness and desires to pass on his vast experience to anyone who wants to step up to the plate. A proud husband, father, and grandfather, Wallace resides in Destin, Flordia.